DREAM WEAVING, DREAM CATCHING, DREAM CHASING, DREAM DOING:

THE SPIRITUAL JOURNEY OF LIVING OUR DREAMS

LISA M. YEZZI, PH.D.

BALBOA.
PRESS
A DIVISION OF HAY HOUSE

Scripture quotations are taken from the King James Version of the Bible.

Balboa Press books may be ordered through booksellers or by contacting:

Balboa Press
A Division of Hay House
1663 Liberty Drive
Bloomington, IN 47403
www.balboapress.com
1 (877) 407-4847

Because of the dynamic nature of the Internet, any web addresses or links contained in this book may have changed since publication and may no longer be valid. The views expressed in this work are solely those of the author and do not necessarily reflect the views of the publisher, and the publisher hereby disclaims any responsibility for them.

The author of this book does not dispense medical advice or prescribe the use of any technique as a form of treatment for physical, emotional, or medical problems without the advice of a physician, either directly or indirectly. The intent of the author is only to offer information of a general nature to help you in your quest for emotional and spiritual well-being. In the event you use any of the information in this book for yourself, which is your constitutional right, the author and the publisher assume no responsibility for your actions.

Any people depicted in stock imagery provided by Getty Images are models, and such images are being used for illustrative purposes only. Certain stock imagery © Getty Images.

Print information available on the last page.

ISBN: 978-1-9822-3004-3 (sc)
ISBN: 978-1-9822-3005-0 (e)

Balboa Press rev. date: 08/27/2019

TABLE OF CONTENTS

DEDICATION

This book is the result of months of open, honest and very vulnerable prayer and meditation that began when I asked God who is my Source and Higher Power, what I would do next.

One day, on a long walk in the woods with my dog, God started to pour the words you are reading into my head. My only job was to transcribe them.

I have done my best. The words are His, the ideas for the Workbook are a result of my combined experience and the ultimate guidance of what or what should not be included to make the message clear.

To my God, the Great Creator, my Source, Spirit and Higher Power, Who has Made a Way- Where there was truly none that I could "see"... My deepest prayer of thanks.

In humble and joyful gratitude for all that I have received.

Lisa

Note: The pages in this book reflect my use of the word God. However, this is a personal spiritual journey and my intent is to refer to each individuals own belief in a Higher Power, a Source, the Great Creator, etc.

INTRODUCTION

In the Beginning…

The most sacred journey that we will ever take is to seek and then live our own dreams. Big, medium or small; each dream is a spiritual gift that reflects our core purpose for being here. Dreams emanate from our soul as a reflection of all that God, our Source, our Great Creator, our Higher Power; has promised each and every one of us. Dreams are our purpose, our mission, our birthright and our duty. To walk through life living large in our dreams is a living testament to all of God's promises.

As we begin our journey and start to talk about dreams and dreaming, hope and possibility enter our hearts and we feel the freedom of life offering us all that we ultimately desire. Dream Doing is not only achievable; it is necessary in order that we fulfill what we have been created to do. Tiny dreams are as important as our largest dreams. Each dream is a part of the vision of the whole of our lives.

Whether we start with dreaming for a new computer, wardrobe, job, promotion, home, career, mission, family or a better relationship- it doesn't matter. Dreaming for health or healing is still dreaming. Wanting new friends, new hobbies, new kitchens, an education, a church community, a stronger spiritual life, or a vacation remains as relevant as any other dream. Dreams are reflection of our own soul and the result of guidance or intuition so that we can take our place in this world and live our lives in peace and freedom. **Dream**

Doing is the ultimate form of respect for our self, for others, and for our God.

Dream Doing is not only for the few; it is for each and every one of us as we take our place in a world that needs what only we have to offer. **Who we are- at our core, is God's gift to us. Who we become is then our own personal gift back to God.** That is why the journey is sacred. It is the act of "becoming" all that we can be. It is our ultimate gift back to our Great Creator, who is our God.

The Nature of Dreams

It seems to be that the nature of dreams is that they are wild, crazy, selfish and non-attainable. We think that only some people have the luck or good fortune to achieve their goals and live their dreams. We think that it is not for us, that we cannot HAVE, and so we either chase only our tiny dreams and suffer through, or we stop chasing any dreams at all and live in total misery. It would seem that we are wrong. It is the very nature of dreams that we all have them. It is also the nature of dreams that they never stop. And here is the worst part of all- *it is within the nature of dreams that they are always within our reach, if we know how to go after them.*

Dream Doing is for everyone and there are a lot of Dream Doers out there sharing their knowledge. Members of the spiritual and scientific community all speak of the same exact process. The advice of theologians, scientists, psychologists and philosophers is out there; ready to be shared with each and every one of us. If we doubt then we need to look at one simple fact…Why is it, that each and every aspect of dream doing is being clearly articulated by people from all walks of life, from all belief systems, from one single source of Wisdom?

Perhaps that is because the one single nature of dreams is that they are doable. Whether small, medium or large, we cannot dream what we cannot accomplish. If a dream comes from our spirit, our soul, our God; it is simply because it is possible.

It is therefore in the nature of dreams that *they come from within us.* No one can give us our dreams. Someone may spark a desire, a thought, a creative surge; but the one thing they cannot do is hand us the dream. That spark only emerged because the dream was there in the first place. It is as personal and individual as we are. It is a total reflection of who we are and who we were born to be.

Just as no one single person, place or thing can "give" us our dreams; *no one person, place or thing can take them away either.* If some of our dreams have been lost, it is because we made the choice to let go of them. It is in the hard acknowledgement of self-responsibility that we will be led to the ultimate freedom. We will learn and then move forward with our new dreams. When we look back within ourselves, it must be with the understanding that it was our responsibility to chase the dream and therefore, it was also our responsibility for taking the next step.

Dreams are consistently moving through our souls. It is our choice whether to listen or not. It is our choice to let big dreams fade into distant memories. It is our choice to try to live straddling two worlds; the world of hopeful possibilities, and the world that we have chosen to create instead. When we take responsibility for the loss of our dreams, we also gain the power in knowing that we have the ability to chase them.

Before we begin, let us think about dreams. One of the first reasons we are here is that we hope to find a way to achieve them. We want them, we see them, and we fear that we will never have them. This is the first limiting belief that often leads us to walk away, to give up, to feel lost and disillusioned. Wanting and not getting is one of the most excruciatingly painful experiences that we can imagine. Therefore we fear that if we dream too much; all we will feel is the deep pain of loss.

This is a negative mindset focused on fear of loss and fear of unworthiness; which is really only a fear of lack of enough of what we need to achieve our dreams. It is a thought, a belief, an attitude, and a lifestyle. It is not reality. It is a limiting belief that keeps us outside of all that we can have. It is a choice, and is subjective. We can change the way we think. We can change what we believe. It is up to us to look at our own limiting beliefs and make the choice to change the way we think and the way we live.

As we take the first step in manifesting our dreams, which is to Become Ready to receive them; we should look to one spiritual law that will help guide us along the way.

God will do for us ONLY what we cannot do for ourselves.

One of the first Actions we will take is to understand the nature of dreams, the spiritual and natural laws that lead to manifestation, and the changes we need to make in the way we think, feel, and act so that we may become ready to create and then achieve them. We will learn what our part is in this process of Dream Doing.

Becoming Ready, Willing and Able

Dream Doing requires us to become ready, willing and able. This is the process that we all follow as we chase our dreams. Therefore...

It is in the nature of dreams that Ready, Willing and Able are spiritual principles reflected in a natural process where each phase is part of a commitment and is integrally related to the next. All other principles and laws, both spiritual and natural, flow from this axiom.

We will begin at the best place we can. We will begin Dream Doing by starting where we are.

GETTING IN SHAPE:

START WITH WHERE YOU ARE

We start with practicing the ART of
Dream Doing on our small dreams.......
And this will be the result ...

**We will face the same obstacles, the same
fears and the same process.**

Enough small dreams achieved and...

**We are building trust in Spiritual Laws as well as Natural Laws
We feel the power of FAITH in "motion"
We are more comfortable with the process of Dream Weaving,
Dream Catching, Dream Chasing and Dream Doing
Through self-reflection, we become more intimate with ourselves
We come to believe
We find more of our true "self"
Our expectations increase
Our confidence increases
Our fear of the unknown process decreases
We learn we are capable
We learn that dreams really can come true
We learn more about responsible choice
We take more ownership of our destiny
We gain strength in the power of commitment
We are more likely to take risks
We learn about the support offered by dream partners
We learn that our perspectives of lack are not the reality
We learn that choices really do exist
We gain the power of positive thinking**

We find gratitude
We see the possibilities
We learn to listen to God through prayer and meditation
We gain faith, trust and hope in our quest for more
We learn another critical lesson- there is always enough of what
we need to get to where we are going.

Let us Begin

THE FIRST STEP-BECOMING READY

It is in the nature of dreams that we are subject to the Spiritual Principle of Becoming Ready.

In order to *Achieve* our dreams, we must *be ready to Receive* them. When we are finally *ready to receive* we will feel freedom from fear and "*Allow*" our dreams to unfold.

We will receive according to what *we feel we deserve.* The spiritual principle of becoming ready is subject to our own willingness to increase our belief in worthiness and deservedness. The only thing that will stop us from achieving our biggest dreams is our unwillingness to believe that we are worthy to receive them. In other words, our dream manifestation is directly related to how much of our dream we are honestly willing to accept.

A fish will only grow to the size of its container. Our dreams will only emerge within the size of the container we choose to provide for them. By designing a small non-deserving container, we box in our dreams and keep them from "growing" to big. We give them limits and boundaries, and then find that our dreams follow those rules. Small containers mean that our biggest dreams will never have the room to emerge to the full size and shape that they were meant to be. Containers are a matter of choice. Ironically, that choice is ours to make.

It is in the nature of dreams, that the more Ready, Willing and Able we become: the more we find that impossible becomes very possible. If we dream it, it is automatically possible.

When we are dreaming large, we often feel doubt and we will certainly hear doubts from non-dreamers. Yet, the spiritual law of intention and dreaming for physical manifestation automatically signals us to God's promises for our life. There is no such thing as impossible. There is only the question of our own deep commitment to be open to receiving our biggest dreams. This commitment grows as our readiness grows.

It is the nature of dreams that they are subject to both spiritual principles and the natural laws of the Universe- since God is the Great Creator of both.

We know now that the science of Quantum Physics has proven some very powerful natural laws having to do with energy. There are books, movies, and articles all sharing the power of this scientific knowledge having to do with the universe. Natural laws designed by God are derivatives of spiritual truths. They are part of, but not bigger than. Because of their origin, they do not work separately; only in concert with each other so that we may gain the power we need to manifest our dreams. We need to understand and use natural law as much as we need to understand and use spiritual principles in the process of dream creation and Dream Doing.

THE NATURE OF INTENT
IN DREAM DOING

It is in the nature of dreams, that physical manifestation is only a representation of the internal voice of the soul.

When we look out into our world, we somehow think that everyone has the same dream. After all, who doesn't want a family, to be loved, to live in a great house, enjoy every day at our job, and of course back that all up with a bunch of cash? This also leads to some idea that since we all dream of the same thing, that we are in a competition, and only some with gain the prize. The prize is as different as the person seeking *it*. There is also plenty of *it*, whatever *it* seems to be for us.

On the surface, what we see are physical manifestations of what we need as human beings. We are born with the needs for food, shelter, clothing and all that it takes to secure them. Basic needs are not dreams. They remain basic survival needs. Survival and dreams are the opposite ends of a very close and private continuum in our own lives. We need to respect the fact that we have needs AND we have dreams. Needs and dreams coexist and remain constant in our lives.

Second, it is the intent behind the dream that differs; the manifestation takes on different meanings to different people. A man sits and dreams of a big house to fulfill his real dream of providing for a large family. A friend dreams of a big kitchen with the intent is to share her love for good food, hospitality and friendship. Another has gone back to school to become an attorney, not seeking fame, riches or glory. She ultimately seeks the pursuit of a just society. An unemployed archeologist spends time digging in the soil to create a community garden in the downtown district because he intends to build a better world. A young man seeks his dream of starting his own business; because his real dream is to design a new way of providing the service that he loves. Another seeks to become a teacher, because teaching is part of his mission.

The physical reality of what many of us seek may look like it is the same. The truth behind the dream is a reflection of each of our own deepest desires. In other words, physical manifestation of any dream is still a representation of the intent of the soul. If one manifestation does not work, then the dreamer finds another way to accomplish the same thing. This is the power of dreams.

It is in the nature of dreams that all of them reflect a personal interconnectedness.

Our dreams are weaved in our souls, felt in our hearts, designed by our minds, only to emerge in our physical world. They are woven from the same cloth, so to speak. The tapestry of our lives will always show it's own personal design, a reflection of who we are in our wholeness. All parts of us are related. We have many dreams, intentions, and motivations, much purpose and clearly we have a mission. Each is personal and individualistic.

If we look deeply and reflect on our lives, common themes emerge and show how interconnected our choices really are. To know ourselves deeply and well, will help to guide us in all of our dream manifestation. The clearer we are in intent, the more faith and trust we will place in ourselves and in God. As we examine who we are, we enter a deeper partnership with God and come to understand that many of the choices that we have made in our lives have been a reflection of our own free will, often dominated by fear, thus, not God's will for us.

It is in the nature of dreams that the biggest dreams we pray for are for the spiritual aspects of intent.

Our biggest prayers are about peace, love, joy, safety, comfort, healing, community, family, compassion, etc. These are dreams of Intent. The manifestation of the dream through prayer will differ according to God's plan for us in our lives. All physical manifestation is concordant with the spiritual intent we seek to increase in our daily lives.

Intentions are reflected in a natural inclination to pursue a lifestyle. Some spiritual intentions are the need to pursue healing, justice, hospitality, nurturance, service, curiosity, music, art, safety, beauty, laughter, comfort, love, belongingness, education and wisdom, to only name a few. Our personal intentions are reflected in the desires of our heart. We each seek our own path through self-awareness and our commitment to realization.

It is in the nature of dreams, that physical manifestation is only a representation of the intent of the soul.

Therefore, each and every dream realized is actually multi-faceted. If we search for only one specific way to achieve our dreams, then we have lost the point. We've also probably lost the dream. Our larger dreams especially are not specific, nor are they subject to certain manifestation. To dream to be a healer does not imply any specific vocation, career or business opportunity- it implies all of them as they are related to dreaming.

We search for The Answer, without realizing that we never asked the question first. Our search becomes haphazard and scattered, spreading the myth of the dream seeker as one who cannot find their way. In fact, our confusion actually relates to our erroneous belief that there is only one right way- and apparently we never read the manual first.

We think that dreams are succinct, linear and rule-based. We seek to find the right way, thinking that if we do, the journey will be easy. When we walk in that direction, we find ourselves lost, because we are. We have no trust in our intuition, no faith in ourselves and therefore, no real faith in our God. We feel that all is subject to some earthly set of standards and rules and that our Creator is capricious, only sending us mixed messages in order to continually delight in our frustrated efforts to achieve that which we want most.

It is in the nature of dreams that the spiritual power resides within the intent, not necessarily within the doing.

All actions on our part are physical because we are physical beings. All manifestations are physical because we live in a physical world. We all "see" what is created as we live our dreams. What we do not see is what is most important. The only thing that matters in the end is the intent behind the doing.

God always knows our intentions, whether we recognize them or not. Intent is the spiritual reflection of God. God cannot be fooled, bargained with, or bribed. Promises to God are one thing; manipulation through promises are quite another. A lot of people do the "right things" for the wrong reason. When intent matches the cries of our soul, then we manifest a representation of God's powerful grace and His plan for our lives.

It is in the spiritual nature of dreams; that we will find ourselves driven to move in a certain direction. These are our biggest prayers, prayers that reflect all of the intentions of God.

These are the dreams that reflect the most powerful and faithful act that we can possibly engage in. Dreams of Intent are the highest form of prayer because in order to be true to them we must have surrendered to God's will. We must have been willing to give up control of our minute understanding and vision of what the dream "looks like". We must have been willing to Let Go, Detach, and allow God free reign in designing our destiny.

Dreams of Intent are the deepest reflection of our connection with God. They are what I call- Wrap Around Dreams. They wrap their arms around everything we need and want. They are top-down dreams. Dreams of Intent are reflected in Praying Big, and then Praying even Bigger...

When we dream and pray on Intent, we do not see, nor do we speak of details at first. We wait for the details and pray only for the clarity we need. We leave that to God in total faith and trust- the gifts of surrendering to His Will. We live in the Knowingness- that we are loved, we are safe, and that God provides more for us than we can ever provide for ourselves. We realize that God gives us our intentions. They come from Him and represent His presence on Earth. We know that God helps us physically manifest any representation of Intent.

It is in the nature of dreams, that the highest order of dreams-mission and purpose; is a call for us to self-actualize.

Intentions are spiritually manifested as we use the gifts, talents and abilities we have each been individually gifted with. We are ready for self-actualization when we have examined ourselves long enough to see our smallest pieces and our largest pieces and celebrate who we are as a whole human being regardless of the feedback we may have received in the past.

Self-actualization is about living in mission and purpose with clear intent to manifest all that we have been empowered to do. It is a place of humility because it resides only in the Truth of all we have been given and all we have to share, offer or contribute. The Truth is found in all of the promises provided when we were born. To recognize, celebrate and embrace who we are keeps us on the path of the purpose for our existence and the mission that we have been asked to accomplish. Truthful self-actualization reflects pure gifted Intent.

We dream free and we live free as we come to know that since these dreams flow from Intent, they are endless. In this sense, the power of Intent leads to many different physical ways to manifest our dreams. We are born with more than one intention, so that we can live a spirit-full life. Spiritual Intent is our purpose. Manifestation is the closest connection and partnership that we can establish with God.

To become ready, we must realize that we deserve and are worthy to follow all of the intentions that we were given at birth.

God Does His Part and He Asks Us to Do Ours

Let's see...if God is actually sending us a dream-shouldn't He also hand it to us as well? I mean, if all we talk about is God's amazing power and what He offers us, shouldn't I also talk about faith as total expectation of a powerful Santa Claus God; or perhaps the God as Aladdin and his magic lamp, or perhaps the Knight in Shining Armor God? Or perhaps, we may think of Him as the April Fool's Joke God- you know, that one- the one who gives us the promise, then jumps out screaming Hah, Hah- joke on you for falling for it!

You may feel that this is an insulting way to talk about God or to talk about ourselves, but quite frankly these analogies do speak to what most of us truly believe whether we chose to admit to it or not.

Yet, God is the one sitting back and saying, I placed it in your soul. I give you the guidance that you need and a system to keep you on track (intuition). I give you ears to listen and a heart to receive. I give you the abilities, gifts, talents and then finally, all of the experiences you need to develop the skills that will help you achieve your dreams. I give you the opportunity to see my plan through visualizing it. I give you my grace through divine intervention, meaningful coincidence, serendipity, and synchronicity- whatever you choose to call my Open Doors. I give you all- except Faith, Trust, Deservedness, Willingness and Fortitude. That is your part, to take the actions necessary to fulfill your dreams.

The biggest obstacle God ever asks us to face is our own fear, in order that we may walk through to the other side and freely embrace Faith and Trust- not only in God, but also in our self. It is in becoming ready that we begin to face and overcome our personal fears as we start the work involved in challenging them and changing their nature. Fear is our greatest enemy, our most powerful personal challenge, and the basic reason why our dreams are not being easily manifested.

It is in the nature of dreams, that committing to fulfilling them reflects total obedience to God.

If God sends us our dreams we then must be obedient to them in order to be obedient to God's plan. Our dreams are God's will for us; which means that we are already worthy to receive them.

As hard as it may be to let go of people, places, things, fears, and prior beliefs regarding self-indulgence, we must let go. As hard as it may be, this is how we practice the highest forms of hope, faith and trust in our God. This is what we have been called to do. This is what makes the journey sacred.

It is in the nature of dreams, that How… questions are related to God's part and not to ours.

The most fear-based question we often ask ourselves up front is "How do I think I can do it?" That simple question kills more dreams than any other. The answer is simple. That's God's job. He always provides the way, even if it seems there is no way, at least not one that we can see at the moment. Just because we are limited in what we can see happening down the road, does not mean that the answer won't be there. It means we have to have faith that the way will be provided. That's God's job, not ours. So, we need to leave the how up to God and shoulder only our own responsibility.

It is in the nature of dreams, that we become highly creative and start generating the What IF? scenarios at a rapid rate.

This leads me to the second scariest series of questions we ask which always begin with What If…? For those of you who believe you are not creative, the 'what if' questions are proof that you are wrong. 'What if' questions are generated by fear-based energy. We create our own nightmares. We create more fear than the fear we started with. We get so obsessive, and let our creative mind run so wild, that we generate "what ifs?" at lightening speed. When we are done; we are no longer afraid, we are terrified.

Our job is to stop using our right brain to create nightmare problems and instead focus it on generating dreams and possibilities. Used properly, our right brain can lead us to highly creative solutions, when we do face an obstacle. We need to save it and use it for its intended purpose. Our job is to monitor and then focus on letting go of obsessive worry. Most of what we create wouldn't happen anyway, so all we are doing is losing precious time and stressing ourselves out to the max.

If we can't let go on our own, then we offer it over to our God. He will gladly take that obsessive fear and burden of worry from us.

It is the nature of dreams, that with each one we receive and achieve; more follow in form and nature, so that the supply is never-ending.

When we choose to follow even the smallest of dreams our risk is minimal. We have the clear and easy path of achieving them. Each achieved, leads us to the next. We may suspect that we are insatiable, but the converse is true. We are building, brick by brick. We are experiencing the Law of Abundance and become increasingly open to the practice of allowing.

Each time we receive the smallest dream we dream again. Enough experience in achieving our smallest dreams, and we dream bigger and bigger. Then we accomplish those dreams. And then do you know what we receive? We hear God saying, "Now it's about asking for more." God has an endless supply and all He calls us to do, is to continue in faith and trust to ask for more of what He wants to give us.

When dreams come from God (who represents eternal abundance), and we are open to receiving them, we find ourselves living within the context of unlimited offerings. That in effect becomes our journey. We walk and talk to God and ask about what we want. Then we pray and meditate, first upon the question and then the answer. We find that our dreams have purpose.

Through prayer and meditation we experience the powerful, positive energy to achieve them, always knowing that the Plan for us is so big that we will probably never see all of it at first. We will experience it and then we will "see" it.

Dreams Have Their Own Essence and Some Have Their Own Time

It is in the nature of dreams that they are constant companions and represent never-ending possibilities.

They begin in our earliest moments, and continue until the day we die. They are not the hubris of the young. Big dreams are not tied to a specific decade or time-span; they evolve and shift within the constraints of time. Some of the biggest dreams we have will show themselves well later, when experience and wisdom tempers impatience and risk-taking. Some of our biggest dreams only emerge after we have already lived a big life. They are ageless and timeless.

It is in the nature of dreams, that our biggest dreams will have this way of sticking to us, until the end of days. That is, of course, only if we refuse to fulfill them.

Here is the truth- our soul never dies. Because our soul never dies, neither do our dreams. Well at least the big ones of course. We may try to kill them and give up on them, we may give minimal effort and then quit, we may listen to others who say dreams do not come true, grow up and get with it. But they remain…

We speak the language of the left-brain and say in all rational adult language that they are unachievable. And as we speak, they so become. It is unfortunate, because as much as our mind said to us- "won't happen for me"…our heart spoke and said "please try"… and our soul continued the journey of reminding us that that is what "we were meant to do". The result of course is such total and complete misery that the next choice is to share what we have come to "believe". Our great gift to others is no longer what we are born to do. It becomes the word of someone who has chosen an alternate path and therefore shares the pain of missed opportunities and poor choices with anyone who cares to listen.

It is in the nature of dreams that many exist within partnership.

Many of our biggest dreams exist within the context of partnership. Partnership dreams are energized by two or more people and because of that they are huge. They take one person's dreams and match them with another's. The spiritual intent behind a partnership dream may differ, but the manifestation of the dream remains the same. The positive energy created by the active contribution of two or more people is so incredibly powerful, that a partnership dream is more easily achievable than most.

Partnership dreams exist in the bonds of marriage, friendship, love, or parenting. Obviously they exist within careers and businesses. They also exist within vocation.

Many people who are Dream Doers spend time with other Dream Doers in a partnership of support. These are very powerful relationships often speeding up the process of dream manifestation. Once again, the positive energy generated by these relationships is synergistic. The contribution of each member in partnership creates energy that is bigger and greater and more powerful and substantial then each member alone can offer.

Partnership dreams also have an additional quality. In order to dream "bigger", both partners must participate; since the energy of only one person cannot sustain a partnership dream on its own. Commitment within partnership dreams is a healthy choice made by two or more people. Therefore, when we partner with other people in Dream Doing, we also face the fact that these relationships may be subject to loss over time.

Even if they are not lost, we would do well to seek God as a dream partner to join our team. The spiritual energy residing within this active partnership role is of course the most powerful energy there is. In *The Power of Positive Thinking*, Norman Vincent Peale consistently reminds us to seek partnership with God. On a daily basis, bringing God into the partnership to play an active role, as mentor and guide will lead us to a greater awareness of where we are to go and what we are to do. If you do not have a Dream Partner or are not involved in a Dream Partnership with others, then focus more heavily on asking God to be your Dream Partner.

It is in the nature of dreams that some of the manifestations must follow time. It is in the nature of Dream Doing that we also face living through Dream Passages. It is in the nature of dreams that endings are always the mark of beginnings.

Sometimes our dreams do not come to pass in the time they were meant to occur. Other times, dreams manifested and then became subject to the passage of time. The dream came and then passed. We cannot regain those specific dreams because they lived within a certain period. There is perhaps nothing more painful in life, then the loss of a long-cherished dream.

There are many dreams that are subject to time. Careers, health, marriages, parenting and partnerships are some of the most significant. Some are subject to the natural law of time. Some dream passages occur because a partner has decided they no longer share the dream. Some dream passages occur because of other people's choices, and that choice directly affects us. Some passages are related to events or perhaps the area in which we live. Some dreams are just created to be finite.

Not one dream passage marks the end of dreams. It leaves space for new ones. As in all dream passages, we cannot give up on future dreams because of the passage of time. If we gave our entire heart and soul to a dream that seems to be now lost, the least we can do is turn to our heart and our soul with compassion. All we can do is respect the loss of those dreams through mourning them, and then move into the acceptance that follows healing. It is then that the new dreams begin to emerge. Dreaming is a continuous process of creating and therefore, as one ends another begins.

It is in the nature of dreams that timing is subject to both spiritual and natural laws.

In faith, we realize that much is up to God's timing. When it is in His time, dreams will evolve. However, we need to be more astute as to what that means. Dream Weaving, Dream Catching, Dream Chasing and Dream Doing are a process. Each part of the creative process calls us to be Ready, Willing and Able to receive what God is offering at that particular moment in time. God immediately Opens Doors- He doesn't sit around waiting until the last minute. Doors open consistently; but with our eye on the final picture, we can miss all of the Open Doors along the way. Because we don't understand what we need, or the best way to support us in achieving our dreams; we don't see the connection between God's Open Doors, and our big dreams.

In dream manifestation, we need to become ready first. As the timing is right, God gives us the opportunity (an Open Door) to learn, to grow, to increase our sense of deservedness, in other words, to become more ready. God is working consistently in our lives. We think of timing as the grand finale "Open Door", when all that we want is presented to us. Often we pray and pray, thinking that God is not hearing us in our prayers or that in effect we must continue to Wait.

Yet God is making ready on His end. He continues to intercede on our behalf, to help make us ready and He is doing the same thing on the other end. He is making others ready. We are not being asked to wait, we are being asked to Act, by walking through the doors that He offers us at this time.

Sometimes we are not ready as I said. Sometimes, He is making another person or place ready and so we wait for that. Sometimes, He is putting things in order so that we may find an easier path. Have you ever been at the right place but it was the wrong time? Perhaps that is more of a result of our own attempts to control timing than anything else. Time is fluid and is not marked on a calendar. We think a month is forever, and a dream that takes years is endless, without realizing that spiritual time is not the same as temporal time.

There is also another natural law regarding timing and people, places and things. God sends us Open Doors through the physical universe- through other people, places, and events. This is the natural law of meaningful coincidence or synchronicity. However, as much as He promises to open a door we need to realize that He is not going to pick us up, carry us over the threshold and plunk us down on the other side. That timing is all about us.

God Opens Doors and we might choose, often out of fear or lack of clarity to walk through the door. God opens another, again urging us to move. Our gut, our intuition, if we listened would say to take the leap. But we choose again; not to-for whatever reason. Perhaps all we do is stick our big toe through an opening and then jump back. This is our timing, and we do have a big part in the process of time. Some of the choices are ours alone. It is not all God. If we do not make that choice, then we cannot say there was no Open Door. All we can say is that we made the choice not to walk through it, at that point in time.

God will continue to Open Doors as long as we continue to seek them. We need to learn from our past mistakes so as not to repeat the same ones in the future. God doesn't get tired, but we will.

If we seek the miracle of God doing all the work while we sit back and keep praying that He does it for us, we will get tired. We will give up. Of all of the people I have met who had doors swing so wide open it was hard to miss- yet still made the choice to turn around and go backward, it is hard to find one who takes ownership of their personal choice. They claim instead that it wasn't "exactly" the open door that they were looking for. They still sit on the couch and wait for the day that God shows them their dreams. They want what they want in the manner that they described it- down to the very last minute detail. And so, they sit, pray, lament, feel self-pity: and refuse to get off the couch and do their part in the process.

Dream Doing Asks Us to Live Whole:
Body, Mind, Heart and Soul

It is the nature of dreams that although they emanate from our soul, they are felt in our heart, give energy to our body through passion, and finally challenge our minds to achieve them. Dreams ask us to live whole: body, mind, heart and soul or spirit.

Dream Weaving, Dream Catching, Dream Chasing and Dream Doing are a creative lifestyle that involves each and every aspect of our being. We will not easily achieve dreams when we are living fragmented lives. We cannot embrace a dream while we are dismissing our heart, ignoring our intuition or abusing our body. We cannot achieve our dreams if we engage in core limiting beliefs. We cannot only think our way into a dream and have the whole picture. We may think our way into a piece of it, but it will never be enough. The dream process is a whole process because that is how we are meant to live. We need to nurture and respect our bodies, minds, hearts and souls in order to gain the powerful positive energy that each contributes to the process.

It is in the nature of human dreams that we feel we need to consistently ASK; but in the spiritual sense of dreams it is GOD WHO IS ASKING US- to search, to find, to receive, to share and then to finally rejoice and therefore witness His presence.

God started this whole process by asking us to follow His plan for our lives. He is the ultimate and consummate Dream Weaver. When we don't listen, or we falter; He just sends constant reminders like this sudden bleeping IM on our computer. Here I am, God is talking-I asked you to become a healer, a designer of a better way, a person to challenge wrong, a parent to guide and love, a teacher to pass on wisdom, a member of my community to pass on faith. I asked you to nurture other souls, to provide the comfort, safety and sanctity of community to others. I keep asking....

Through spirit or soul God created a direct connection to our spiritual essence, to the core of whom He created in hopes that we would find His Way. But then it got better. He connected us to a heart, so that we might feel His presence. Then he gave us a physical body to move and continually show His Presence to the world. Finally, He gave us a mind in order that we may find His wisdom and set out to follow it. He offered the gift of a whole body, so that we might have the ability to feel the wholeness of all that He offers us each day that we walk this Earth. Dreams never stop coming, because God never stops asking.

It is in the nature of dreams, that since they are spiritual, they are innocently played out in childhood games, interests and hobbies. In dream recovery, we often find the core.

Childhood games and dreams are a reflection of our emergent self. As children, freely open to our souls and our creative right brain; with no adult constraints dictated by any reality - we play and explore within our core. Children only play with ideas that ring true to them, or that interest, challenge and delight them. All children engage differently in dream play because of the individual nature of the dreams that emerge. As children, there is little differentiation of self; children live holistically rather than in fragments. That is one of the reasons why children explore dreams so freely. There are no boundaries, limits or rules in a child's world. As adults, we wish for the same freedoms.

It is something to examine. If we seek to know what interests us- look back to what used to interest us- and in the end we will find our core. Forgotten perhaps, but far from lost. Old dreams are retrievable with enough effort. Assets are recovered as we clarify childhood dreams. Dream recovery leads to the re-emergence of long forgotten dreams and lost gifts and abilities. All of these remain.

It is in the nature of dreams that we are given all of the gifts, strengths, talents and abilities to achieve them. It is in the nature of humans that somehow we think that our goal is to live life trying hard to overcome our inherent weaknesses.

Our first, and highest goal is to establish all that God gave us at birth to work with. These are our assets. He intended us to use them.

God makes us ready, and also gives us a subset of abilities and the experience needed to become skilled. He does this so that we can live whole. In order to achieve our highest dreams, we must become cognizant of our true abilities, strengths, interests, skills and experiences. They were intentionally gifted to us. It is time that we become open to discovering our gifts so that we may now choose to embrace and use them.

God never asked us to live in our weaknesses to prove that we are worthy. He is perfection and we are not. To live in our weaknesses, trying hard each day to become great at them is worship of perfectionism. It is the act of trying to create a Fake Self; one that pleases the outside world yet keeps us in constant inner turmoil. It is emanating from fear of unworthiness.

This choice of lifestyle is a definitive representation of blindness to all we have been given. It is clearly not worship of God and actually represents living in the darkness. Since perfectionism doesn't exist except with God, this approach will continue to lead us to focus on a non-achievable goal. These are not dreams. We are stressing our bodies, losing our minds, breaking our hearts and killing our souls. Somehow, spiritual redemption is not a part of what we are doing. We are not reflecting the grace of God if this is the path that we have chosen to follow.

It is the nature of dreams that not each and every aspect of our dreams is about making money. It is also in the nature of dreams, that many of our dreams are about living well rather than accumulating more...

It is interesting that somehow we believe that every dream should have a cash value to it in order to be worth our time and effort. It is not the nature of dreams, which are spiritual to be about cold hard cash. But, we often make our choices based on money, rather than turning inward towards the true meaning of our existence.

Dreams in terms of work well done do produce money, because when we do what we are born to do, we will do it well. With faith, we will do it great! We will live in passion and the energy will be more than what anyone could imagine! Money follows our dreams. The Universe has an abundance of money.

The fact that we have basic needs and a responsibility to ensure our survival is definitely a natural law. We need to have our basic needs met, and met well. It is our birthright, not some exceptional privilege. If one of our core beliefs is that we need to sacrifice our dreams in order to provide for our basic needs, then it is time to get over it.

Spiritual and natural law have many stated givens, and this happens to be one of them. God knows that we need food, shelter, medical care, clothing, work, respect, love and belongingness because He is the one who created us and gave us those needs. There is no mystery about basic needs and our right to ensure them. Chasing dreams does not get in the way of basic needs; it seeks to fulfill them and move beyond. To live well and whole and joyous and free is the essential core motivation behind seeking and living our dreams. That is the spiritual energy that drives us forward.

It is the nature of dreams that to live outside them is to survive and face challenges, but to live within them is to truly live large regardless of challenges.

There is not one human being on earth that will live life without facing pain, suffering and the inevitable challenges that life presents. But, the difference in the quality of life lies in our choice to either survive in fragmented parts, or to live holistically and balanced in our own dreams.

Life energy is renewable because it is spiritual, positive, creative and generative. It is there, if we choose it, to support all of our efforts. To live in our dreams is to renew our energy each day so that we are prepared to face any obstacle or challenge that comes our way. Living our dreams offers us quality of life. Survival is just survival. Daily we are faced with the same question- should I choose to survive? Or should I choose to live?

It is in the nature of dreams that it takes more energy to survive outside of our dreams than it takes to live within them.

There may be those times in our life when we face a fork in the road, when left represents enduring never-ending 24-hour periods, and right represents the fear of risk and the challenges that represents.

It is here, that we are asked to make a decision. God remains at our side, no matter which way we choose to go, but clearly offers us the path to fulfilling the dreams that are part of our being.

When we start each day with the mindset that it will be a chore, rather than a chance we live outside our dreams. When we endure each day, facing all of the obstacles and never seeing the opportunities, we have used vast amounts of life energy just to survive. Surviving outside our dreams is the greatest of hardships. Living our dreams is the most faithful life we can possibly imagine. The challenge is in the 'crossing over'.

It is the nature of dreams that they may, in fact, touch off the healing that is necessary to achieve them.

For those of us who need to heal our hearts, minds, souls and/or bodies, we are given the opportunity within this process to do what needs to be done. Without healing, we will never be able to sustain ourselves on the dream journey. We must heal whole, to dream big and thus live. We may, while we are healing continue to work on our dreams and achieve them, but healing is also a part of our big dream. It will be done as we continue on. We may fear it, and we may attempt to avoid it, but we will never stop it.

Living whole gives us a stronger sense of intuition, an ability to freely tap into our creative right brain, the physical life energy that will sustain the effort and the joy when our heart feels that we are 'on track'. Dreams touch off healing as part of the process. It is natural and healthy. It is a significant spiritual gift when this opportunity is offered to us.

It is in the nature of dreams that healed trauma survivors have more within them to achieve than anyone else on Earth.

Trauma survivors are closest to my heart. I am one and I know many. One of the many assets of a trauma survivor is the will to carry on- to fight- and so the spirit is strong and able. As trauma survivors, we have seen the face of darkness and have learned to go on despite it, precisely because we have had glimpses of the light. That is what is to survive. To have faced the worst and survived it means that we have all the ability in the world to create and achieve our dreams.

We have seen the worst and overcome. We can envision the best and know that our fighting spirits will carry us the rest of the way. We know what it takes to survive and we know we are capable. We fear less of life precisely because we have experienced more. We clearly don't want or need a repeat and that is natural. But we are capable and we know that too. We have survived and healed and therefore we know in our hearts and souls that people, places or things cannot beat us. We are gifted with the knowledge that we can do whatever it takes. A healed trauma survivor who taps into God's continuing presence is formidable.

The Size of Our Dreams

It is in the nature of dreams that they come in all sizes, shapes, colors, and smells. It is in the nature of dreams to constantly grow and evolve.

Dreams have no boundaries. They are limitless and so they evolve, change, shift and consistently grow. Dreams are an act of creation, no matter what the size or shape. They are always about thinking outside the box, only because they are too big to be contained. There are no inherent walls or limits. Even the smallest dream, wish or desire is about building something new.

It is in the nature of small and medium dreams; that they consistently witness and testify to God's presence on a daily basis. Achieving small and medium dreams reflects joy in acts of God in day-to-day living.

Each time we feel the gratitude in the accomplishment of a small or medium dream we have the opportunity to grow in faith and trust. On a personal level, this is huge and a great shift on our part. In gratitude we practice the spiritual act of joyful receiving through active recognition of each gift, small or large. We become practiced so that we increase our faith because we have seen and experienced Dream Doing in our daily lives.

It is in the nature of dreams, even the smallest dream, that the resulting energy is always generative.

Little dreams captured contribute to our wholeness as a human being. No dream is too small to be considered. Think of it. Our smallest dream will make us smile, give us the gift of joy and fill us with gratitude. So what do we do? We follow up with random acts of kindness (another spiritual gift). We generate more of what we have received.

We hold a door, step back in line, smile and wish someone else a great day. We allow someone access on a busy street. We stop long enough to listen, and offer what we can. We sit in peace and share that with those around us. We generate the joy and significance that accompany our meaningful presence with others.

Since every dream, no matter the size is a true reflection of who we are- we share our truth with others. It is, as always, in the small things that we do that show people who we truly are. We share all of the qualities of dreams with others and generate the positive energy that flows with them. Our positive energy has now enhanced at least one moment in another person's life.

It is in the nature of dreams that small and medium are generally about basic needs, wants, wishes and desires. Our biggest dreams are about self-actualization: mission and purpose.

It is in the nature of dreams, that although some are small and seemingly insignificant, it also takes small effort and little risk to achieve them. The gift in achieving small and medium dreams is that we are learning how to get to the big ones. It is therefore in the nature of dreams that all are important, each in their own way.

Each small and medium dream achieved deepens our faith and trust in our God and our self. Each small step fights our fears and chips away at our limiting beliefs. Each time we achieve, we find a greater sense of deservedness.

If we sacrifice small and medium dreams thinking that this is the way to manifesting larger dreams, then all we experience is the powerful limiting belief of lack. When we see and then do not receive our small and medium dreams, we sacrifice gratitude, joy, positive thinking, and feelings of abundance. We pay a huge price when we deny ourselves to such an extent.

As we limit ourselves in accessing abundance, we also choose to limit God in his ability to provide all that He has to offer us. Choosing lack will only create more lack in our lives. We are not being spiritually humble or noble; we are acting as if we are not deserving of even the smallest dreams that God has offered to give us.

It is the nature of dreams, that living within them changes our lives at the smallest level. It is the nature of dreams that each time one is achieved our lives are shifted to a new level of joyful awareness.

We wake up each day invigorated, excited, content, and happy- or at the very least, totally capable of getting there.

We look forward to living within the dream each and every day.

We face the day with any inevitable challenges seeing and knowing that there is resolution. We stop focusing on the problem, and start living in the solution. We even know what that means.

We offer a physical sense of positive, passionate, and creative energy to the world. We receive the same in kind.

We are not as prone to the plethora of distractions offered in our world. We need less sleep, we understand how to keep ourselves in balance and consistently challenge ourselves to enlarge our dreams and create new ones. We have come to know what it is like to respect ourselves enough to live whole.

We love what we do and we are good at it. We focus on being true to ourselves. We feel the humility in being blessed and privileged by our freedom to stand tall in our own truth.

We are intimate with our own self. We know that we have something to share with others and love the opportunity to contribute, to give back. We offer our time, our treasure and/ or our talent in joy that we have been given the opportunity to do so. We attract more of the same into our own lives.

We are positive and therefore attract positive people to us. We are positive, and negative people seek us out to find their own answers.

Each moment of the day, we are deeply grateful for all that we have been given, and all that we are about to receive. In gratitude we find deservedness. In deservedness we find more opportunity.

This is what it is to live our dreams. This is what it is to live in total connection with God, following His guidance, His plan, His offering to us.

It is the Nature of Dreams that they remain a clear and obvious representation of our morals, values, ethics and internal beliefs. It is in the nature of dream living that we find our own humanity.

Priming The Pump

If I could freely indulge myself...I would

_____

_____

If I could freely indulge myself...I would

_____

_____

If I could freely indulge myself...I would

_____

_____

If I could freely indulge myself...I would

_____

_____

If I could freely indulge myself...I would

_____

_____

If I could freely indulge myself...I would

_____

_____

If I could freely indulge myself...I would

_____

_____

If I could freely indulge myself...I would

_____

_____

If I could freely indulge myself...I would

_____

_____

Lisa M. Yezzi, Ph.D.

Dreams and Intent

My Heart's Desires:
What Makes My Heart Sing...
(Create your own List)

WE WILL ALWAYS FIND WHAT
WE EXPECT TO FIND

WE can ask for anything in the world, but the majority of the time, we will receive exactly what we unconsciously expect to receive.

List at least one time that you ASKED in HOPE for something, secretly praying that the outcome would not be what you truly expected it to be. In other words, you hoped against hope that this time it would be different. But it wasn't- the outcome was exactly what you expected it to be.

Now, write down one time that you got exactly what you asked and hoped for even though you never expected that. How did you classify that? As luck? As one of "those Moments"? As great, but just not enough?

Lisa M. Yezzi, Ph.D.

First Pray Big- and then Pray BIGGER
idea from the Book- <u>The Prayer of Jabez: Breaking</u>
<u>Through to the Blessed Life</u> by Bruce Wilkinson

DEAR GOD

I Pray for

I Pray for

I Pray for

I Pray for

I Pray for

I Pray for

I Pray for

I Pray for

I Pray for

I Pray for

I Pray for

And then- I PRAY BIGGER

Gratitude List
Each day, Give God thanks for _20_
moments you were grateful for

Dear God, today I am grateful for

Dear God, today I am grateful for

Dear God, today I am grateful for

Dear God, today I am grateful for

Dear God, today I am grateful for

Dear God, today I am grateful for

Dear God, today I am grateful for

Dear God, today I am grateful for

One of the most common practices of all dream doers, positive thinkers and spiritual leaders is the daily expression of gratitude to God for all they have been given within the day. No matter how your day goes, you will be able to find 20 distinct moments in time that you can be grateful for. The power of this simple daily prayer is immense. To increase the power of gratitude, always write a list. Write it out by hand for the greatest effect.

Lisa M. Yezzi, Ph.D.

Childhood Dream Recovery

What games did you like to play when you were young? (games also include sports)

What kinds of people, places or things peaked your interest?

What hobbies did you enjoy- or did you desire to engage in?

What challenged you and peaked your interest?

What kinds of things delighted you?

Name some of your favorite childhood places...

My Personal Sources of Positive Energy

People

Rituals

Places

Activities

My Dream Weaving Web

Create a Dream List or a Dream Journal

As each dream manifests, cross it off your list
Include small dreams, wishes, wants and desires....

Have Fun!!

1. _____
2. _____
3. _____
4. _____
5. _____
6. _____
7. _____
8. _____
9. _____
10. _____
11. _____
12. _____
13. _____
14. _____
15. _____
16. _____
17. _____
18. _____
19. _____
20. _____

This activity comes from Julia Cameron- the idea is that by writing our dreams, we will be closer to manifesting them.

My Personal List of Fears

I am afraid that. . .

_____

_____

I fear that. . .

_____

_____

What if. . .

_____

_____

How will I. . .

_____

_____

I think that. . .

_____

_____

I am even more afraid of. . .

_____

_____

I am not certain about. . .

_____

_____

And I am also afraid of. . .

The Greatest Challenge God will ever ask of us- is to both face and then walk through our own fears...

<u>Circle</u> every single fear that has to do with lack. Rewrite each lack statement as an abundance statement.
<u>Star</u> the HOW fears and write a list to offer those to God who will always take care of all of those needs and fears.

Lack to Abundance:

Dear God- Here's that Fear List You Wanted

Notes

THE SECOND STEP-
BECOMING WILLING

It is in the nature of dreams that we are subject to the Spiritual Principle of Becoming Willing.

We start the journey of willingness by being open to possibilities. We start by being open to the power of all that is revealed to us in Dream Weaving, and the hope that this is the beginning of the path to achieving our dreams.

Willingness goes beyond being open and non-judgmental. It requires us to commit to exploring a new way of thinking and believing. Willingness extends to being aware that living life in a holistic and therefore balanced way is within our grasp. It means acknowledgement of the idea that perhaps the way we normally think, feel and act is not helping us. We then move towards the willingness to consider making some changes. Willingness is a form of commitment to our self and is a journey in its own right. Starting with Dream Weaving and Dream Catching, the positive power of willingness grows and requires more from us.

Later, we become willing to go to any lengths to Do IT- whatever we decide IT is. We become open to surrendering control to God and to all of His power. We become willing to detach from all that is not servicing us in following our dreams. We become willing to let go of some people, places and things (like our old ideas) that continually stand in our way. We become willing to be open to hope, faith and trust. In that sense, we become willing to walk through our fears, each of them, one by one. This is a huge commitment, not to be taken lightly. Spiritually, we must become willing to walk in the dark, with no knowledge of what lays ahead, only our faith and trust in God, our Higher Power, that we are being directed on the right path.

It is in the nature of dreams that hope springs eternal.

Hope is a huge sign of willingness. It springs eternal, because it will remain with us until the end of days. Hope is God's signal to us to look once more, to seek the possibilities, to see in clarity what we may have missed, to catch what is new, and to begin to dream again. Small, medium, or large- all dreams are nourished by the richness of hope. It is the energy that resides in faith, the one single consistent source of energy that can keep us going forward.

It is in the nature of dreams, that to become willing we must become open to surrendering to God's plan for us.

Many of us don't understand what true spiritual surrender means. We think that to surrender to God and His plan for us requires that we live a live of martyrdom and loss; base survival at best. But that is the opposite of what we do surrender to.

God planted dreams in our hearts and souls so that we might find a way to live happy, joyous and free. In that kind of lifestyle we witness and testify to His intent. To surrender to God means that we give up our own meager attempts at control and ask if we can join in partnership with Him.

It is not about hardship, it is in fact a journey through fear and towards great joy and freedom. To surrender to God's will, simply put- is to commit to doing whatever it takes to realize the dreams that He has planted in our souls. A major part of the journey will be our commitment towards becoming willing and open to all that is offered to us.

Dream Weaving, Dream Catching, Dream Chasing, Dream Doing- the Creative Process

It is the nature of dreams that they are the act of full creation. It then follows, that it is the nature of dreams that they will follow the laws of God and nature. It is the nature of dreams that they come full circle.

Dream Doing is a process. It is a process that must be followed to achieve product. As in all processes, it is recursive rather than linear. For most of us, the non-linear fruition of dreams is our greatest challenge. For others, the recursive and circular process of Dream Doing makes total sense. In either case, it remains true; in order to get to a product (our dream), we must move through the Creative Process (Dream Weaving, Dream Catching, Dream Chasing, Dream Doing) to get there.

It is in the nature of dreams that God- the Greatest Creator has gifted us with the Creative Process- so that we may be guided in the act of creation of that which He intends.

There is no mystery to the Creative Process. It has been used for centuries by researchers, scientists, artists, engineers, psychologists, inventors, philosophers, theologians, gardeners, decorators, cooks, physicians, mechanics, builders, teachers, children, peacekeepers, parents, partners, dreamers and doers. They all followed the same simple steps, whether they were aware of them or not. The Creative Process follows a very simple and straightforward method that has now been recorded and is easily understood. It is a natural law that most acts of creation emerge by following the same few steps. All we need to know in creating a dream is to understand the steps involved in the Creative Process.

It is in the nature of dreams that our part is first to perceive them and then to achieve them.

God's part in all of this is to send us our dreams. Our part is to become open to perceiving them. In Dream Weaving and Dream Catching, we show our willingness to perceive all that is offered. The next step is achieving them.

The ultimate joy of a dream is in our feelings as we fulfill it and therefore cherish it. The journey, the work involved from beginning to end is the source of our passion and the ability to always do that much more. What all of us love most is the feeling of honest achievement. It is what drives us forward, what propels our day, what leads us into peaceful, yet joyful expectations of our tomorrows.

First, there is the Creative Process that will help guide us in achieving our goals.

Although there is a list of stages; this does not imply that they occur in order, nor are they achieved in a step-by-step fashion. We do not start with the first step, finish it and then move on to the second step, clearly finish it and then sprint off to the third. The nature of the creative process is that it is recursive, which is circular rather than linear. To experience the power of the Creative Process means that we need to let go of some 1,2,3, off to the finish line idea.

Second, most members of our society sorely misunderstand the word creative. We describe people as being creative, with no knowledge of what that means. We say- this one Has it, and this one Doesn't. We contrast our efforts to the creative expression of another person. In comparison someone always comes up short. The act of comparing shows ignorance of the powerful nature of individualistic acts of creation.

We are all creative, each and every one of us. We are all equally creative, each and every one of us. Had a great nightmare lately? Sat and ruminated about all the possible events that may happen in the future, and scare your self to death lately? Well, there we go. We each share the power of creative thinking, it's just that some of us are more willing to accept the idea and describe ourselves as creative. Those of us who consider ourselves to be creative then think and therefore act creatively. It is then, a matter of thinking differently in order to practice differently. It is not a matter of gifts. (There is such a thing as right brain vs. left brain dominance, but we will discuss that later).

It is in the nature of dreams, that Dream Weaving always starts the process of perceiving and that Dream Doing is the general

process of achieving, and that there are several places we will visit in between the two.

The steps of the Creative Process that I will use come from the Writing Process, because many of us are familiar with the terms. If you enjoy science, then link the stages with The Scientific Method. They are the same, just a reflection of different labels.

Dream Weaving

The first stage of the Creative Process is called Pre-Write or Brainstorming. It is the free generation of all possibilities. We do not think, evaluate or judge. We pick something and just go with it. Every single idea that comes to mind will be written down. The more that is written, the easier dreams will evolve later. This is Dream Weaving. It is spiritual and therefore intuitive. There is no right, just as there is no wrong. Every single idea has the same value as the next.

Dream Catching

Once we feel that we have done enough Dream Weaving- we move to Dream Catching. This is when we look at our list and let our heart and intuition chose all the ideas that we would like to Chase. Sometimes, one idea will spark another and we end up back in Dream Weaving- allowing ideas to grow and thus, generate new and related ideas. Sometimes, we have enough, and move forward.

This stage is like a first draft. We perceive it as a work in progress. We know that there will be future revision. First drafts are never final stage. They are rough around the edges. They are generated without censoring if we really want a great product in the end.

First drafts, Dream Catching- is more about following the pieces of the dream a little longer to see where they lead. Later, we may want to embellish certain pieces. Or we may want to put some of them on hold. Later we may totally discard pieces of it. Those decisions in the Dream Doing Process are best left for a time when our choices are based on the best possible course of action. At this point, our first draft- our Dream Catching is not subject to logical analysis. That logic we are so fond of can kill a good dream before it even has the chance to emerge.

Dream Weaving and Dream Catching continue on at an increased rate until our dreams are ready to be fairly well defined and we move into Dream Chasing.

Dream Chasing

In the writing process, when we are ready, we move to second draft, where we take our first and begin to edit, move and shift. In Dream Chasing, this is the point where we start to make choices about what dreams, or aspects of our dreams we would like to chase in this moment in time. We delete ideas that do not work within the framework of the Dream Chasing that we have delineated.

Dream Chasing is more logical than Dream Catching. It works on patterns and creates wholeness. It sees parts as related to wholes. It defines what appears to be the strongest of all of the possibilities. In Dream Chasing, when ideas coming from the first draft of Dream Catching don't work, we go back to brainstorming, using Dream Weaving to create additional possibilities for the dreams we have chosen to pursue. We play with possibilities in order to create the kind of ideas that will lead us to a better product, or a better way to achieve it. We use Dream Weaving to fill in the gaps that are now missing, as we clearly become Dream Chasers.

Dream Weaving and Dream Catching at this point, continue, but at a decreased level until we call them back into play during the Dream Doing stage. When we face obstacles that require weaving and catching, we return again to the origin, the creation of possibilities.

Dream Doing

Dream Doing is the final draft. It is the plan. Once here, we are working on a logical way to accomplish our dreams. In Dream Doing, we often look back to our first and second draft for ideas we may have missed, for a new perspective, for a stronger approach. Dream Doers always go back to Dream Weaving in order to generate all the new possibilities needed to fulfill dreams. Dream Weaving is a strong, spiritual and intuitive way to solve problems or create a way around any obstacles that lie in our path.

Dream Doing is a journey, it doesn't happen in a day. It happens over time. The larger the dream, the longer it may take to evolve in it's wholeness- especially, our Wrap Around Dreams. We live each day in Dream Doing when we dream that big.

Dream Doers use the creative process to build their dreams and create their new reality. This is not an instant act, where the perfect dream evolves in its wholeness. It is not a process of throwing spitballs at the wall and hoping somehow one of them will stick. It is an active, involved, spiritual and natural process that creates a new and unique whole out of all we offer to put into it. The process is subject to its own time. There is no rushing through. Many wonderful dreams took longer to weave and catch then they did to actually Do. Other dreams take longer in the Doing. The process is recursive, but not subject to time. It starts when it starts and it really never ends. Recursive is circular- there is no beginning and no end to the dream process unless we choose to create one.

Dream Weaving...Dream Catching...

For many of us, Dream Weaving and Dream Catching will be our greatest challenge. We don't tend to "think" that way. We don't tend to use our intuition as a guide to dreaming at all. We are not skilled at right brain activity because school, work, and often life have taught us that this is a waste of time. We are left brain focused, because the world has taught us to be.

Let us look at Dream Weaving and Dream Catching in a broad sense before we dismiss the process or find it too challenging. Remember, the process of weaving, catching, chasing and doing is recursive, or circular- a complete reflection of the act of creation and a process that follows the law of nature. Even those who follow the ideas of science and the natural laws of energy that exist in the Universe talk about the Creative Process and refer to each of us as creators (e.g. Byrnes, Dyer).

It is in the nature of Dream Doing that the creative process is subject to the natural Law of Attraction.

The Creative Process is linked to the Law of Attraction. It makes sense, if we stop to think about it. The idea is that we attract whatever we believe we will receive. The creative process is subject to the Law of Attraction, because as we become open to new and original thoughts and ideas- we find that we generate even more of them. Creating creates increased creation, so to speak. Like ideas follow like ideas.

In *The Secret*, the natural Law of Attraction is highlighted as one of the most important of universal truths. The premise is that we will attract into our life what it is that we are thinking about. If we are thinking fear-based thoughts, we will attract fearful events. If we are open to thinking creatively, we will attract the positive ideas and solutions that we seek.

In *Positive Imaging: The Powerful Way to Change Your Life,* Norman Vincent Peale mentions the same idea- that thoughts influence what happens in our lives. He also mentions the powerful connection between our thoughts and our emotions. In other words, if we believe there is no way, we will feel defeated, and we will find failure every way we turn. We will suffer through the experience of defeat, because that was the negative energy source we were using to create our dreams.

In the *Bible*, we are told to Seek and we shall Find. If we seek new ideas, we find new ideas. If we seek abundance of time; we will find an abundance of time. If we seek positive support; we will find it. In order to create a new life, to live in our dreams, we must totally believe and then, act accordingly. We need to take positive action through positive thoughts that create positive energy; that then attracts additional positive energy and events back into our life.

The constructivist psychologists believe that we create our own reality. How we perceive life and live within it is a product of our own thinking. Many scholars, psychologists, theologians and scientists will say the same thing. What we think, leads to how we feel, which leads to how we act, which leads to choices that generally confirm what we thought in the first place. We continually try to change our lives by doing the same thing over and over again- each time, expecting a different result.

We run in circles until we change our thinking, and the energy that was behind the thought. When we choose to believe in self and then in our dreams, we will achieve them. The creative process is positive energy and will attract more positive energy to us. We are, as the constructivists say, creating our new reality.

It is in the nature of Dream Weaving that it often occurs best when we are alone, or we are relaxed enough to "hear the still, small voice within"; as it urges us to consider new ideas.

Dream Weaving and Dream Catching are spiritual, intuitive, and therefore deeply personal and intimate acts. We tend to Dream Weave and Dream Catch when we are alone, relaxed, and not censored by our own self-talk, or by the talk of others. Highly creative people often get their best ideas in the shower, upon waking in the morning, while taking a walk alone (my preference is in a natural surrounding), while driving a car, when listening to music, when writing, when jogging, when quietly meditating after prayer, etc. It is in these moments of quiet that we most easily move into our spiritual or intuitive side. We also, start to access our right brain- the seat of intellectual creativity.

These activities as well as others allow us to access our creative intellect. In other words, they allow us to move into right brain thinking. In the 1970's research by Sperry sparked the beginning of our understanding of the distinct roles that each side of our brain plays in intellectual functioning. Our right brain is our creative side. It is non-verbal. The jobs of the right brain include the creative generation of new ideas and behaviors. The right brain is emotional and visual. It allows us to see the big picture. Our right brain creates a new whole out of all of the parts of what we are dreaming about. It is intuitive, rather than objective.

To be able to access the full capabilities of this part of our brain is the goal of Dream Weaving. To be able to generate all possibilities, we move to our creative side and begin to think much differently. Using all the possible strategies we can to access our right hemisphere when we are in the Creative Process leads us into a more powerful position in achieving our dreams.

Creative artists and Dream Doers in all areas of life use Dream Weaving as a process necessary to achieve their goals. As Michael Gelb relates in *How to Think Like Leonardo da Vinci*, even the great artist, scientist, inventor, engineer, philosopher himself, said that he consistently took time to relax and let his ideas about a project continually grow. In other words, da Vinci always took the time to Dream Weave when he was doing his work. The creative process is the same, regardless of who chooses to use it.

It is in the nature of dreams that Dream Weaving has it's own spiritual purpose. It extends all the possibilities of dreams that we may chase in the beginning and it also extends all the possibilities that will help us achieve our dreams at the end.

Dream Weaving is like a tapestry made of thread. If a thread is broken, a new one is picked up to replace it- showing a slight deviation from the original plan. Yet the basic pattern of the tapestry, the weaving, remains intact.

This is the essence of the Dream Weaving that we will experience. It is the deepest understanding of our dreams and being open to the process that is attempting to weave them. We will not achieve each and every one of our dreams in the exact manner we have dictated. We may find that it emerges in a slightly different color, but is always consistent with the same theme. The theme is our essence, our own Truth, the final manifestation of Intent.

If we allow true Dream Weaving, we will not deviate from that path. No matter the challenges, the passages, the loss we may face, when we move into acceptance- a new, extended version of the same basic dream begins to weave a new pattern, and so our dreams continue on. When we remain open to Dream Weaving we also open the door to Dream Catching. We allow our dreams to evolve and shift- knowing that core dreams are never lost in the process.

It is in the nature of big dreams, that they are limitless. It is in the nature of Dream Weaving that we tap into the natural Law of Abundance.

Think of a backyard, a really big one. What is the first thing we think about as human beings? We think containment, through gardens, trees, or fencing. We think about limits, because we want to live outside of the fear of lack of control. Big dreams are bigger than us; the power is so huge that we often seek to control it. Any perception of lack of control appears to feel overwhelming, jarring and totally out of balance.

Bigger than us is not logical, not easily understood or categorized. Big dreams continue to challenge, and then to escape us. We seek containment, for all the wrong reasons. When we try to control Dream Weaving in order to seek containment; we only limit God and the abundance He attempts to share with us through the creative process, especially in Dream Weaving. We become entrenched in the fear that we are little fish and we want the safety of a really small fish bowl.

Dream Weaving, done with an open heart and mind shows us the power of limitless abundance, at both the beginning of the process and once again at the end. We are little fish until we throw ourselves into the big pond. We seek all that a large pond has to offer us, and we grow in the process.

It is in the nature of Dream Weaving and Dream Chasing, that as we tap into the natural Laws of Abundance and Attraction; the Creative Process increases in strength and power as it moves us towards achieving our dreams.

Dream Weaving taps our soul into the power of total, unlimited abundance. This is the power of Dream Weaving and Dream Catching; if we are open and willing to engage in the process.

The natural Law Of Abundance coincides with the Law of Attraction through the commitment in our acts of allowing our creative energy to flow. In *The Artist's Way: A Spiritual Path to Higher Creativity*, Julia Cameron states that creativity is a part of life energy and that by tapping into that source, we find a spiritual path that connects us to God. Creative energy, which we generate through the Creative Process, is then, a positive, natural and innate source of energy. The more that we use this universal source of energy, the more we attract into our lives. In other words, the more we create; the more we become able to create.

The Law of Abundance states that there is no limit to positive creative energy. There is also no limit to whatever we need to take our creative ideas and make them a physical reality. There is plenty of whatever we need out there. There are plenty of ideas, friends, mentors, houses, vacation spots, etc. There is plenty of time, money, work and support. It is there, all of it, in total and complete abundance, waiting for us to grab on and go with it.

We have a human tendency to focus on lack. There are no jobs, there is no time, there isn't enough money, there aren't any good support systems.... on and on we go- focusing on the lack of good ideas, or the lack of people to share them with. If only... becomes our daily mantra.

Once again, the Law of Abundance is a law that is related to belief and positive thinking. It is a positive flow of energy through the universe, and the universe has plenty to share. We cannot have 'it' if we think 'it' isn't there for us.

All the great spiritual and religious leaders, scientists, psychologists, dream doers, etc. speak clearly about the power of understanding, thinking and acting as if there is plenty and it's coming our way. Visualization is a way to manifest our dreams in a clearly positive way. The power of visualization is well known. We allow ourselves the freedom to live our dreams in detail. Become willing to accept the idea, as hard as it may be, that once we create and then visualize our dreams, they exist. If we allow that level of faith to enter our subconscious, then we can express gratitude for the fact that our dreams already exist. And they do, because we have captured them and can see them. Be grateful; because the positive energy and law of attraction will now step in even further in helping us physically manifest all that we "see". We have started to catch our dreams.

It is in the nature of dreams, that as we Dream Catch- we Dream Commit.

As we catch- we show our willingness to commit. This is the act of choice, a powerful energy that resonates though our hearts, our minds and our souls. Once caught our dreams become part of us. We listen and we follow. This is a purposeful and a conscious action on our part. We consider it joyful, just building our ideas; continuing to weave and then catch all that are related. We are willing to be open… and the possibilities enlarge our vision even more.

It is in the nature of dreams that Dream Catching is part of the intuitive process and in that sense retains its spiritual nature.

When we look at all of the possibilities that we create in Dream Weaving and start the process of choosing the ones we want to focus on; we make an active choice. It is not as mindful as it is intuitive and emotional. We start to make choices that bring us joy. We feel the flow of positive energy and want more.

This part of the process remains tied to our spiritual nature. When we let intuition guide us, and feel the result in our hearts- we are tied to spiritual choice. The time for logical decisions will come, but at the earliest stages of Dream Catching we are best served by going with our intuition and then our heart while we Dream Catch.

What Science and Psychology Have Shown Us
<u>Getting in Our Own Way</u>:

It is both a spiritual and a natural law, that in order to manifest our dreams, we are better served by living whole. It is also true that by living our dreams, we will find ourselves living whole as one of the outcomes of Dream Doing. The process creates and re-creates and builds upon itself.

Think about this one truth…

A lot of people build dreams and are unable to maintain them. Then they finally stop and give up altogether. As sad as this story is, you know it is the truth. You do not have to live whole in order to achieve your dreams, but in the end, you will need to live balanced in order to build upon them and continue to manifest them in your life. Forget about the money people, the stars, and all of the doers we don't even know. The truth in the end is that if we are not connected within- to our bodies, hearts, minds and souls we will be working at a deficit. And we will continue to struggle all our lives to make up for it, no matter what the outside world sees. They do not see us. We do not see the internal world of others. Dreams may emanate from our soul, but they need the rest of us there to manifest and to maintain. End of story…

Towards that end, we must be willing to heal whole. That means getting rid of old baggage, examining and discarding limiting beliefs, focusing on the actual truth of our assets so that we might discover them, realizing our limitations in truth rather than choosing to belief in that old self-fulfilling prophecy, addressing the effects of our life style on our bodies, and finally healing our hearts through this process.

Is in the nature of dreams, that positive begets positive- and that negative vs. positive deters and sometimes kills the dream.

When dreams emanate from our soul, they are always full of positive energy. When we try and achieve them surrounded by people, places or things that only carry negative energy, then we must remain guarded. Toxic energy is negative energy and is focused entirely on destruction. We must never look to negative energy for support and collaboration in dream development. We must avoid the Nay Sayers, the Dream Slayers and the Dream Killers, in order to finally achieve our dreams. We must only seek out other Dream Doers and Dream Partners, in order to support our own journey and in return support theirs. When we turn to those who only see lack and failure, we find in their energy the focus on lack and failure. This is not what we need to achieve our dreams. In the end, all we do here is spend endless energy trying to talk someone else into being positive and therefore believing in our dream. If they don't believe in the beginning, they will never be there at the end. And anyway, it is not worth losing our dream in hopes that in time we can talk someone else into believing in it. The only one who needs to believe in our dream in the beginning- is us.

It is in the nature of Dream Doing, that we will encounter Nay Sayers, Dream Slayers and Dream Killers.

It is also in the nature of dreams that the only power that can stop our dreams from happening is OUR OWN. We cannot seek Nay Sayers, Dream Slayers or Dream Killers to help support us in achieving our dreams. We can kill our dreams all by ourselves *or* in the company of others. The choice remains ours. Remember the Law of Attraction. If we are negative- we will attract negative people, places and events into our lives. Like always begets like.

The Nay Sayers

The most dangerous Nay Sayers are the little voices that chat away in our own heads that continually tell us we can't do it…

The Nay Sayers that are the most damaging of all are the voices we hold in our minds; the ones that we continually pull out and use against ourselves. They were born in the past and if we are smart we will choose to let them remain there.

The Nay Sayers are all the limiting beliefs that we have come to call our own truth. They are the culmination of the voices of people, places and things that let us know that we just were not really quite worthy. We were too tall or short, too slow or fast, too loud or quiet, too deficient, too lazy, too selfish, too messy, too plain, too reflective-well, you know- so obviously "less than"…

They are the voices that *we have adopted and chosen* **in time** *to believe*. They are the ones who said creative ideas were crazy or disruptive, or insane or just plain dumb. They were the ones who said we would never have; because we were non-deserving, no matter what we did. They are the ones who now occupy a huge space in our lives called the Self-fulfilling Prophecy.

The Self-fulfilling Prophecy

As a long time educator, I saw the result of this powerfully destructive idea play out in the minds, hearts and souls of more children then I would dare to count. If it was hard to challenge the core beliefs of a child, you can begin to imagine the difficulty as an adult.

A prophecy is a prediction. As children, when significant others in our world told us "who we were", they then created a prophecy of our lives. The idea of the Self-fulfilling Prophecy is this- as children we learned to fulfill that prediction. The prophecy of our life as determined by others was seen as "truth".

The self-fulfilling prophecy states that we will seek and then find any type of evidence that supports the core beliefs about ourselves that were given to us as gifts when we were children, teenagers or young adults. We will seek and we will find, each and every one- as proof of "who we are"- regardless of the amount of evidence to the contrary. When are were told negative things about who we are- we walk with blinders on- seeing nothing but the *so-called truth* told by a fallible, social-arbitrary world of people, places and things.

Nay Sayers then are all of the limiting beliefs; thoughts and ideas that we have accumulated that PROVE we are limited and defective in some fashion or another. When we keep a mindful focus on our perceived deficits, we never examine our gifts. When we live within those boundaries and call them truths- we will say no to our dreams and we will learn to accept the unacceptable. We will move through life without challenging core beliefs that are not even true!!!!!

The past can be quite burdensome- it can hold us down with huge weights, and keep us struggling to just keep our head above water. When we look to support from our own Nay Sayers, other people who are Nay Sayers, Dream Slayers or Dream Killers - we are trying to create positive solutions using all negative energy. We must look within and pull out all of those old negative ideas so that we can see them in the light and establish the fact that they were never true.

Paddling or free style- sink or swim. And in the meantime, believe this- if internally we are saying "no way" to our own dreams, we will easily absorb the idea of "no way" from other negative thinkers. The double no way message is a real whammy. The law of attraction just loves that one, how much more negative can we get! Regardless of the law of attraction, the power of the self-fulfilling prophecy assures us of the result.

In addition, any other mistaken beliefs we have about others or our world is an additional piece of baggage. When we believe what is false- we pay the price. Ideas of lack, for example- are all Nay Sayer baggage that keeps us from even making a worthy attempt. If you say *"I don't have enough of..."* you have engaged in the destructive act of Nay Saying. And as you look around your little corner of the world, all you will ever "see, think, feel" and therefore experience, will be lack.

The Dream Slayers

Dream Slayers are not feelings. Feelings are fleeting, they come and they go freely. Dream Slayers are emotional states of being that are the result of negative core beliefs, ideas or thoughts (the nay sayers). Dream Slayers are the way we live life and interpret it in an emotional sense. It is our social- emotional view of the world. Emotional states of being are always fueled by the negative energy of fear. These states accompany us constantly, whether we are aware of them or not.

Nurtured by our Nay Sayers, that constant chattering that feeds our core beliefs about who we are - emotional states of being include; doubt, lack of trust in ourselves, often in others, sometimes in God, shame, guilt, blame, inferiority or low self-esteem, a feeling of being emotionally isolated from others, feeling stuck or stagnant in our lives and finally, despair. If we define ourselves as unworthy, we live in these emotional states of being, and we surround ourselves with people, places and things that mirror our own belief system.

Just out of curiosity- if the Dream Slayers are hanging out- How do we come to feel Deserving???? And **if** in fact, we get some sense of deservedness, how far do you think we can willingly be open to accepting and allowing our dreams to even emerge?

The Dream Killers

The Dream Killers can affect each and every one of us. It does not matter how positive we may personally feel or how far we have traveled in achieving our dreams. Dream Killers exist outside of us. They can be other people, places or things that are toxic, destructive and keep us from achieving our goals.

Dream Killers generate all the fearful possibilities that make our lives unmanageable. Although fear naturally lives within each and every one of us- the Dream Killers continue to help us remain focused on it. They are the fertilizer that nourishes our fears and allows them to grow wildly out of control. They cannot create fear; they can only heighten it. This is their power.

No one single person who is doing or living a dream is walking through life *without fear.* They are doing it *despite* their own fears.

Dream Killers (people) have had the personal experience of killing their own dreams, and willingly share their inevitable misery with us. They may not be clear about their past. They may claim that they have achieved their own dreams. They may even believe it themselves. They may act as if they are only there to help and guide us so that we will more safely move along the path. They are manipulative, negative, controlling, and toxic.

People can be toxic, but so can places we frequent or activities we choose to engage in. Lifestyle choices can be toxic and kill dreams as well. If we obsessively worry, compulsively act, or consistently engage in some sort of addictive lifestyle; we are at risk of killing our dreams. Whether socially accepted or not; obsessive thinking, compulsive behaviors and addictive lifestyles are all destructive and toxic. Each of them is built on fear.

Dream Killers can show up in the beginning, when we are just opening up to our possibilities. They hang out and minimize or criticize our efforts. They show up in the middle and tell us that achieving only the tiniest of dreams is our reality. They challenge us while we are chasing our dreams, with fearful possibilities: therefore, diminishing our energy, faith or hope. Or they show up at the end; sharing their concerns that such "luck" won't last forever, and so we should be grateful for what we have in the moment. They also can appear when we have finally achieved our dreams. Letting Dream Killers in then and holding on tight to them will lead us to lose our dreams later.

If we are full of Nay Sayers- we need to challenge and change the way we think.

If we live life in Dream Slayer states of emotion, changing the way we think will help us change the way we see and therefore feel about life.

If toxic people, places and/ or things currently surround us, we need to evaluate whether to include them in our Dream Doing lifestyle. In many cases, these Dream Killers should be left behind. As hard as that may be, the responsibility of healthy choice is left in our hands alone.

It is in the nature of dreams, that we must practice containment. We need to establish limits, boundaries and other healthy ways to protect our emerging ideas.

If you do not want to share your ideas with others- don't. They are very personal and intimate, especially during the wide-open period of Dream Weaving and Dream Catching. If you do want to share your ideas, make sure it's with another Dream Doer- who will validate and support your efforts in every positive way possible. Do not look to others to "give YOU" positive feedback, because you are scared, unsure or feeling like a crazy person. Sharing our dreams as we weave and catch should only be done in an environment of full trust. Violation of our dreams at this point can be deadly.

Right Brain- Left Brain
The functions of each side of our brain

Jobs of the Right Brain	Jobs of the Left Brain
Emotional- feelings and fear	Logical
Pictures- images	Language- words
Wholes and the relationships between parts	Parts and specific details
Synthesis- taking all the parts and creating a new whole	Analysis- taking a whole and breaking it into parts

(According to Bloom's taxonomy-Analysis must occur before synthesis)

Holistic thinking	Sequential thinking-
Linear sequencing	
Time free- may lose a sense of time altogether	Time Bound- has a sense of time and goals and our relation to those goals
Creative- in terms of new ideas and patterns of behavior	Creative- in areas of language
Memory: Faces, Music, Visual	Memory: Language for e.g. Stories, Names
Intuitive	Objective
Non-verbal	Verbal

The Creative Process

Dream Weaving-   RB only

Brainstorming only- there can be no judgment, no conscious evaluation as ideas flow onto the paper. We do not evaluate here, we generate all possibilities in total freedom.

Dream Catching-   RB dominant

Look at your web- highlight all the ideas that grab you. Move quickly. This is intuitive and emotional.

Dream Chasing-   LB dominant, RB secondary- available for intuitive needs and to generate possible solutions. Out of all the highlighted ideas, star the ones that you feel you want to "chase" right now. This is more logical and analytical but there is still NO judgment. It is important in Dream Chasing that we keep ourselves in LB as much as possible. The job of the RB is to continue on with possibilities- it will stay in Dream Weaving forever, if we allow that.

Dream Doing-   LB dominant, RB secondary- available for intuitive needs and to generate possible solutions.

Set up an Action Plan- use all the abilities of your Left Brain in order to achieve a solid working plan.

Go back to earlier stages as necessary to build a solid Action Plan.

When our right brain works in partnership with our left brain; we achieve the balance that we need to be successful.

It is Critical to Remember- this is not linear- you will need to go back to Dream Weaving and Dream Catching and Dream Chasing all along the path of Dream Doing. The creative process is recursive, which gives it its power to achieve goals and build dreams.

The Creative Process is also used in Dream Maintenance.
Once achieved, we will continually need to refresh, rebuild, and create new solutions as obstacles occur. The process defined here allows us to continue on our path of living our dreams.

Whole "Self" Assessment

Where are you when you get your "best, and most creative" ideas?
High creatives consistently seek stimulation and know themselves well enough to follow through.

Describe your daily energy cycle. What times of the day are your most productive, relaxed, tired, energized, efficient at tasks?

Early morning
Late morning
Lunch time
Early afternoon
Late afternoon
Early evening
Late evening

What do you do weekly ......
For fun
For relaxation

For enjoyment
(creative inspiration comes to us when we are either doing something fun, or we are doing something that we enjoy)

What is the cause of the most stress in your life at this time?

What do you do to reduce that stress?

What do you do daily, weekly or monthly to nurture your whole self? (body, mind, heart, spirit).

Physically, I take care of myself by....

Mentally, I take care of myself by....

Emotionally, I take care of myself by....

Spiritually, I take care of myself by....

Asset Recovery/ Limitations Discovery

List your TRUE Assets Here:

_____
_____
_____
_____
_____
_____
_____
_____
_____
_____
_____
_____
_____

List You're your TRUE Limitations Here:

_____
_____
_____
_____
_____
_____
_____
_____
_____
_____
_____
_____
_____

Asset Recovery/Limitations Discovery

LB activity- look at your asset column and see what assets can be used to compensate for limitations- circle them and cross off the corresponding limitations.

RB activity- look at the list of limitations that are left. Now make a list of all the possible ways (using other people, places, or things) to compensate for each limitation.

Limitations	Compensations- People, Places, Things

How We Perceive Life Becomes Our Own Reality

What we BELIEVE (what we think)

Leads to …How we FEEL …

Which Leads to...How we REACT or The ACTIONS that we take...

The constructivist psychologists state that Mentally We Create Our Own Reality. Spiritual leaders, scientists, philosophers, psychologists- all agree.
SO...
IF we consciously change the way we THINK...
WE WILL automatically change the way we FEEL...
WE WILL then, unconsciously change the way we ACT...
And then New Things Will Come to Us- especially Our Dreams!!!!
(Reminder- what we truly believe is often reflected by what we SAY)

My Nay Sayers

Remember, nay sayers are the voices of people from our past who have defined us as unworthy or deficient in some fashion. Current nay sayers are the people who reacted to our dreams with a condescending smile as if we were either children or lunatics. They were always willing and able to share every reason they could think of as to why our ideas won't work. Present nay sayers validate all the negative core beliefs that we hold from our past.

List all of your current and past Nay Sayers here...

To help with this exercise use your answers from The Power of Limiting Beliefs exercise.

My Dream Slayers

Reminder- Dream Slayers are our own creation. They exist within us. Dream slayers are emotional states of being fed by mistaken negative beliefs (the nay sayers). Write down all of your emotional states of being that are fairly consistent and are getting in your way.

Ideas-
Issues with trust and commitment
Emotional states relating to Doubt, Shame, Mis-Trust, Guilt, Inferiority, Isolation, etc.

My Dream Killers

Reminder- These are people, places and or things, that are toxic in our lives and that have the power to destroy our dreams. List all the possible Dream Killers that exist in your life today.

The Power of Limiting Beliefs
**Many of our dreams, especially our small
ones- are easily achievable.
If we are not manifesting them in our life, we need
to look at how We are getting in our own way.
Limiting beliefs are a reflection of Social-Arbitrary Learning**

My Limiting Beliefs

About Myself   **About My Past**

About My Current   **About Others In My Life Situation**

**Beyond the self-fulfilling prophecy emerges a world perspective.
What we think about our world becomes our reality. Our thoughts
are the most powerful weapons of self-destruction that exist. This
is the key to our level of deservedness... it is the core of the nay
sayers...**

**After reflection: What "ideas" from your past have become your
"truth" today?**

Dream Weaving, Dream Catching, Dream Chasing, Dream Doing:

Acknowledging God's Gifts To Us

My Special Gifts   My Own Experiences

My Unique Set of Skills   My Special Talents

My Special Interests

Who we are is God's Gift to us…
Who **we Become** by accepting and using all that He has given us…
Is how **we Gift ourselves back** to God…

Stop and Smell the Roses

A Gratitude List

Gratitude is really all about seeing God's amazing power and grace in every moment of our day. Stop and smell the roses, watch the sunset, the eagle fly in freedom, the skies open up in refreshing rain, the rainbow at the end of the storm…and then give a word of Thanks.

Dream Recovery

If you were told that you only had one year to live and you had the freedom and the money to do whatever you wanted…

What would you do?

My Dream Catching Web

THE THIRD STEP- BECOMING ABLE

It is in the nature of dreams that we are subject to the Spiritual Principle of Becoming Able.

It is time. We have been working to become ready and deserving of our dreams. We have practiced being open and willing to generate all the possibilities and the hopes that accompany them. It is now time to become able; so that we receive all that we deserve.

Becoming Able is a mixture of all of that has come before. In becoming able we blend spiritual practice with natural processes. We are at the stage of manifesting our dreams. We are building on our foundation of faith, hope and trust, as we Dream Chase and Dream Do.

As we move into Dream Chasing and Dream Doing; we are beginning to refine our search and commit to clear goals and objectives. We will be faced with obstacles and we will often be challenged to find creative and novel approaches to solving them. We will design a way to follow our plan.

Becoming Able is a period where we practice living in a very balanced manner. We need to use our logical mind and our creative mind. We will be most successful by following our intuition when it guides us in a certain direction. We will find that channeling our creative energy in the most productive way we can, will keep us from feeling overwhelmed and exhausted.

To become able to Dream Do is made easier by following spiritual principles, natural laws and the processes and techniques that we

71

know work. In Dream Doing, doors will be opening. Creative energy will increase as we continue to engage in the Creative Process. We will focus on believing that the Dream exists- because we have prayed *and become ready and willing to receive it*. We will continue with prayer and meditation, gratitude and positive thinking. We will believe in abundance and continue to attract more of it into our lives. We will allow God to do His job and practice patience, letting go, surrender and non-attachment to outcome. We will allow the dream to emerge, in its own time and physical essence. We will find that the promises are a reality. We will become Dream Doers in the biggest sense of the word.

Dream Chasing, Dream Doing and The Creative Process

It is in the nature of dreams, that becoming able requires us to continue on with Dream Chasing and Dream Doing.

Here we are- we are getting close; so close we can feel it. It is a scary time and an exciting one, all wrapped up in the dreaming process.

Much of the time that we spend in Dream Chasing is in refining and reaffirming the validity of many of the pieces of our dreams. We are chasing down all the parts that we need to finish before we can really do the dream. Perhaps we are considering details, or eliminating ideas that are not part of the whole picture, or perhaps acquiring the knowledge we need to push through to the end. Sometimes we are facing obstacles on our path and need to go back to Dream Weaving to seek out all the possible solutions to the dilemma at hand. The Creative Process is fully recursive during this final period of Dream Doing.

Dream Doing requires us to use every tool we have at our disposal in order to achieve our goals. The Creative Process is only embellished when we focus on our assets and bring in the support of others to help us along the way.

It is in the nature of dreams, that Asset Recovery will help us achieve our goals.

What is a "liquid asset"?

Think about it, the question is important. As we have worked to discover our assets, we now work to "recover" or "restore" them. When we face obstacles in our path including fear of failure; our intimate knowledge of our strengths, gifts, talents, experiences and skills will help guide us forward. What about our true deficits? Understanding our *true* limitations, what we are naturally not good at, gives us the freedom to ask someone else to come in and use their gifts to help us overcome or compensate for our natural and normal limitations.

When we are totally honest, we are humble and therefore we are living in our Own Truth. Our assets have become liquid; fluid and flowing to the betterment of our Dream Doing. When we can lay down our defenses and honestly say we are not good at this, that or the next thing; we know this is fine, because we are good at this or that or something else. We have now increased our strength, because we have achieved balance through truthful self-awareness.

If God put us on Earth to share our assets with others, then our own judgment of their significance is meaningless. So, stop focusing on your limitations and stop minimizing your assets. It is not truthful and is pure negative energy.

List your true assets and make a plan to use them in order to maximize your own power in achieving your goals. Take a look at your true limitations, and clearly evaluate whether those limitations are causing you any difficulty. If they are, then generate all the possible ways that you can find the support you need to overcome, and continue on.

Establishing Dream Partnerships

It is in the nature of dreams, that spiritual support is one thing and human support is quite another. Both are necessary. Spiritual principles merge with natural laws. Both are of God.

In order to support our efforts, it is wise to start keeping company with other Dream Weavers and Dream Doers. They walk the same path as we do. We establish respect and belongingness within a community that is like-minded. There are many days during our journey when we will want, need, and should have the support of other people as we move towards our dreams. In seeking support from others we experience the strength of a shared journey. We face the same obstacles, share the same feelings, know the same elation, seek the solutions and become at times confused or overwhelmed by the task at hand. To have someone to talk to who is in the same place is a comfort that can never be underestimated. Dream Doers share their path and mentor us. A Dream Weaver shares her/his personal process. We will not stand alone. With adequate and compassionate support, we will move towards our dreams faster and easier, due in part to the shared power of positive energy that is focused on the Solution.

It is in the nature of dreams, that establishing a support system of dream partners or a dream community of like-minded others will speed us toward our goals.

There are those who say we cannot go it alone (in terms of the support of other people). I do not agree. We can always go it alone, but it really is a more productive and joyful journey in the company of others. Those of us blessed with people-support are most likely to succeed and get to the goal faster than those of us who struggle to achieve alone. Never minimize the power of community in supporting our goals.

It is wise to seek the right partners in achieving our dreams. Dreams are intimate and personal. They are a reflection of who we are at our core level. So naturally, since we seek support, we tend to seek it first from our most intimate relationships. In some cases we would fare much better pitching our ideas to a perfect stranger.

If we are struggling with Dream Doing to begin with, then it is fairly certain that we don't live with Dream Doers. Dream Doers would be constantly challenging us to follow our dreams and supporting us in our efforts. Additionally, intimate dreams and intimate relationships combined, can add up to deep intimate wounding. Intimate relationships are the most powerful relationships that exist. They are at their best when standing beside us and at their worst when they are putting us down. If there is little to no support, if there is nay saying or downright dream killing, then our chances of achieving our goals are moving into the impossible range.

Seek positive Dream Weavers, Dream Chasers and Dream Doers. Share your dreams with them. God made human beings to dream together.

It is in the nature of dreams that in the process of Dream Doing, we will be faced with choices.

Healthy responsible choice is a balancing act. We have a responsibility to ourselves to achieve our dreams. As adults we are often living with others and we have a responsibility to them within that particular relationship. There is often a fine line between healthy and responsible choice and decisions that are not healthy.

Helping others and putting some of our dreams on hold is sometimes a decision we must make. Consistently putting others needs and dreams before our own, is an unhealthy choice that is self-destructive. It is once again, built on fear and negative energy.

In order to help others, there is often a time when our needs and our dreams must come first. In these times, chasing and doing our dreams is the healthy, responsible choice, and we cannot let ourselves get off track. It is a major decision, because regardless of the choice we make, we will live with the consequences.

Who Comes First?

When we travel on an airplane with small children or perhaps someone with an infirmity or disability- we are told that if the oxygen masks drop down, to place one on our self before attending to the needs of others. As a mother often traveling with a young child, I used to look at the stewardess as if she was insane and actually had two heads- neither of which was working properly. As a mother, my instinct was to get the mask on my child first in order to save him. As I look back now, I am sure the stewardess was praying we never needed oxygen masks, because every parent was sending her dagger eyes. And in my need to take care of my son first, both of us would have surely perished.

Sometimes in order to achieve our dreams, we need to leave some people behind. Sometimes our dreams may mean relocation to a new area. Sometimes our dreams just don't include others. Sometimes others choose not to follow us. During Dream Catching; when time, focus, money, change and risk come into play, final decisions must be made.

When you are faced with a decision, think about those O2 masks; pray and meditate before you make a choice and then stick with your conviction. To own our own power requires responsible choice, so that we are able to accept the outcome of any decision we make.

It is in the nature of dreams, that we will often be called to fight the darkness in order to remain in the Light.

We cannot look for answers in the darkness that only exist in the Light. Therefore, part of our challenge will be to "see" the darkness for what it is. It is here that we find the nay sayers, the dream slayers and the dream killers. This is the darkness to which I refer. These situations suck out our life energy. They kill our dreams (our spirit), and therefore they break our hearts. They are clearly not "of God" and His plan for us. We cannot easily achieve the dreams that we seek when we surround and immerse ourselves in the negative energy of self, others, places or things. We will leak out all that we have just to defend ourselves. We can't afford to do that. We need to identify all that gets in our way and then make a plan to live outside of those dark places.

Dreams emerge in the Light and follow the Light. This is how they take seed and grow. It is not in the nature of dreams that darkness is a part of fruition. It is clearly a spiritual directive to go within and start the self-reflection that is necessary to clear the path to a personal realization of all that God asks us to do. The inner strength that comes from a faithful connection is enough to support us and guide us through all the times of adversity.

Establishing Partnership With God

It is in the nature of dreams that as we weave, catch, chase and then do- that we are at the same time strengthening our partnership with God.

In doing our dreams we establish partnership with Him. We never, ever have to stand alone. Some of us take the dream journey in deliberate partnership with God through active choice. Some of us find the strength of this relationship as we move through the process of Dream Doing. Each time we partner with God in manifesting even the tiniest dream, than not only do we receive the dream; we also deepen our spiritual connection. When we partner in full faith and trust with God, we become unstoppable.

It is in the nature of dreams that in order to achieve them, we must master the art of "peaceful" patience. The bigger our dream, the more practice we will be offered.

We often say that our timing is not necessarily God's timing. But one thing that we often do is pray prematurely for God to open the doors of the Universe and guide us into the "done" part of doing. When the doors WE SEEK do not open, we must practice a peaceful state of patience, which is built in faith and trust.

It is human nature to ask before we are ready. If we are not ready, God lets us know, by continuing to guide us into being made ready. He opens other doors. He protects us from ourselves by closing some doors as well.

When we are in partnership with God, timing is partially our responsibility. He will not open the doors before we are ready, willing and able to receive what is on the other side. Patience is not with God per se. Patience is for us, requiring us to peacefully come to a deeper understanding that we are not ready, or the Universe is not ready and that when it is time, we will know. God is not asking us to wait in order to practice patience. He is asking us to wait in order that we may have all that we pray for.

It is in the nature of dreams, that as we are practicing the art of peaceful patience, we must turn inward through prayer and meditation.

We must look inward and ask God through prayer what we need to do in order to move forward. We may find that the answer is that something has been left undone. We may find that we still have some lessons to learn, or that we have not accomplished ready, willing and able in one fashion or another. We also may find that what is holding us back is fear of moving forward. Meditation will give us the answers to our prayers. God will guide us into an understanding of the next steps we must take. In partnership, God will answer our prayers in one fashion or another. If there is something He is doing; He will let us know. If it is something that we need to do, He will let us know that too. Prayer and then Meditation keep our connection open and flowing- for our complete benefit. Peaceful patience allows us to move more comfortably in the direction God asks of us.

Spiritual Principles and Natural Laws

Open Doors

When we ask for the Universe to intercede and provide the way, we are praying for God to show his amazing Grace, Power and His Promises. We ask for manifestation through people, places and things, so that we experience His power in visible, concrete, physical form. As the timing becomes right, it is always there.

In order to realize the power of natural law, it is our job to become open to seeing it. God, through the Universe, is interceding constantly on our behalf. To become increasingly sensitive to this power, we often use prayer, meditation, gratitude, positive thinking, imaging, and visualization.

It is in the nature of dreams, that as we continually commit ourselves, God sends through the Universe all means of support to help us achieve our goals.

One of the great wisdoms shared by other Dream Doers is that what "seemed" impossible became totally possible through meaningful coincidence, synchronicity or by the alternate phrases divine intervention and 'just meant to be'. Doors just keep opening! The spiritual act of fruition is not the result of any force on our part. This is natural law. We don't "make" it happen, we just do our job so that when the day comes that it is meant to be, we are ready. This is called Faith.

Dream Chasing often leads us to one open door after another, as the Universe continues to provide us with all we need to help us achieve our goals. It is a high energy time, very positive and intuitive, as well as logical and planned.

Dream Doing starts to emerge during Dream Chasing. One part of the Action Plan after another gets "checked off" the list. We are focused on moving forward with the knowingness that we are beginning to walk in our dream lifestyle. Open doors continue and we see synchronicity or meaningful coincidences increase. The How questions are answered through the response of the Universe as we remain focused on achieving the physical manifestation of our dreams.

It is in the nature of dreams, that Open Doors, synchronicity, or meaningful coincidence might not be what we expect.

God often speaks to us through people, places and events in our world. He uses the Universe to send the messages we need to hear. If we don't "hear" them the first time; He will send more.

A suggestion, an idea, an obstacle overcome related through a seemingly unrelated series of events…an open door, a closed door, a familiar scenario or one distinctly different that what was expected… are all connections to our lives. The Universe provides us consistently with little hints and big suggestions. Hearts open and reveal a truth we need to hear.

At some point we "hear it", we get "it", we may "like it" or we may "not like it"; or we may be thrown totally off balance. The Universe has done its job. God has our attention.

As a hint- when the still small voice of our gut, intuition, or spirit speaks to us- we would be wise to listen the first time.

The Law of Attraction
It is in the nature of dreams that they are subject to the natural Law Of Attraction.

Scientists have proven the existence of this powerful natural law. Spiritual and religious leaders discuss it. Psychologists, philosophers, artists and educators, as well as Dream Doers focus on the effects of the Law of Attraction. In a simplistic, scientific presentation- this law is about the energy that naturally exists in the Universe. It has been clearly proven that like energy attracts like energy. Thoughts and unconscious beliefs are energy, just as much as our words and actions (for a more detailed explanation, please refer to Byrne, Dyer, Osteen, McNally, Peale, and Cameron in the reference list. There are plenty of other writers out there as well). I urge you to take the time to read and understand this law because it has the power to change our lives and the course of Dream Doing.

It is in the nature of Dream Doing, that the powerful Law of Attraction promises us that we will receive exactly what we expect- no more, no less.

In essence, if we truly believe we are not worthy of our dream, then we will never see it. If we believe we will get our dream, the energy is positive- and our dream materializes. If we believe that something won't work, then it won't. There is an old saying, "Be careful what you wish for, because it will probably come true". Our unconscious beliefs about our world and ourselves are our wishes. They dictate what we say, how we think, how we feel, what we do, or how we react. Whether we realize it or not, this hidden energy is creating our own reality. We can hope, dream, pray and visualize all we want, but the Law of Attraction states emphatically that we will only attract people, places and things into our lives that reflect what we *truly* believe.

Thoughts and beliefs are either positive or negative but are always pure energy. Energy is energy. It cannot be fooled or bargained with. We can pretend all we want, but the energy remains what it is until we purposefully change it.

We might get lucky, and get a piece of our dream in spite of ourselves but we generally can't hang on to it. We don't have the positive belief structure to maintain and build on a dream. We hold on by grasping, clinging and holding our breath in deep fear of impending loss. We get what we are waiting for. We lose our dream.

The Law of Attraction and Self-Reflection

The Law of Attraction leads us to deep self-reflection. We have to look at what we say- because our words reflect our beliefs. For example, if we are constantly apologizing for every single thing we do; it reflects a core belief that we are a burden, the creator of havoc and problems, unworthy of respect, etc. If we consistently blame others or God for every misstep; then we reflect the core belief of a powerless victim. If we judge others harshly, criticize those around us, or share other negative thoughts or actions, we have to look to our core belief about ourselves.

We need to look at the types of choices we have made, because actions speak even louder than words. If we consistently accept jobs that are below our level of competence or that clearly emphasize areas that we are limited in, or we consistently boast about our material possessions, or we chose to stay in a relationship that is hurtful; these actions are a reflection of what we think we deserve. Take a look at your choices, big and small; from how you dress to whom you befriend, to what you do for enjoyment. It speaks volumes of your unconscious beliefs and will help guide you in your excavation.

We reflect in order to find, excavate, challenge and change our core limiting beliefs. We reflect and see the power of the Law of Attraction when we find ourselves living out the lies of the

Self-fulfilling Prophecy. We realize that our lives reflect *who we believe we are*, whether that is generally deserving, or generally not. As we do that, we free ourselves to change our limiting beliefs. The majority of these beliefs aren't even true. We are paying the price because we have chosen to listen to others about who we are. With a negative, non-deserving, worthless, disrespect for our true self; we attract into our lives people, places, events, and things that mirror our own belief. Big dreams can never emerge in that type of toxic energy. All that we do is re-create what we have had in the past.

When we finally excavate, reflect on and challenge our core limiting beliefs, we need to eliminate them. They are deficits and they must be removed. If necessary, seek help from a professional who will help guide you when you are thinking wrong. I would also suggest that you look to your God and pray that He removes them. Turn them over to God, who is more than willing to take them from you. They are burdens and obstacles in our path of achieving our true intent. Then, be on guard for the nay sayers, and extinguish their ongoing messages. Between our efforts and our spiritual willingness to let go of our limiting beliefs, we will move towards the positive energy we need to confidently attract positive people, places and things into our lives.

Positive beliefs create positive energy, which attracts more of the same.

The Law of Abundance

It is in the nature of dreams that each one of us can tap into the Law of Abundance.

God presents us with endless abundance. There is no such thing as a spiritual limitation. We have enough of what we need to achieve all of our dreams. *If we dream it, it is only because it is totally achievable. The physical universe is there, just waiting to provide.* However, if we limit our ideas through a basic feeling of non-worthiness or fear, then we will only limit what we attract into our lives. Limiting is not spiritual, it is human. Focusing on the lack of what we need only attracts more lack. We focus on not having, and we attract more of the same. In other words, seek lack and we will be sure to find lack.

Abundance is clearly related to the Law of Attraction. If we choose to limit our dreams, we choose to limit what God can offer us. We will only receive that which we believe we deserve. *The issue is not lack of abundance; it is the fact that we are limiting our access to what **is already** abundantly there.*

It is in the nature of Dream Doing, that the daily practice of gratitude will extend the power of generativity and lead to continued abundance.

The practice of gratitude is one of the most powerful spiritual processes that we can engage in. Gratitude focuses on abundance rather than lack. The more we practice gratitude, the more abundance we find in our lives. We tap into the Law of Abundance with minimal effort.

Gratitude also taps into the Law of Attraction by extending positive thinking to more areas of our lives. The energy that emerges within us is positive and also generative. It generates more gratitude, which then spills out of us as positive thoughts, beliefs and behaviors. Positive thinking generates more positive energy, which attracts more positive responses from the universe.

In other words, the more we practice gratitude on a daily basis, the more we will bring into our lives to be grateful for. In the beginning, we will start to notice that we are feeling better and more positive. We begin to seek more of what we want, whether in small ways or large. As the practice of gratitude generates more abundance, we believe positively in the powerful energy that it continues to generate.

We start to do more of the "right things" for us, because we are seeking a life of more. We attract then, more positive people, places, events, ideas, and things into our lives. The longer we practice gratitude on a daily basis, the more that will come our way. Gratitude grows in direct proportion to the energy we put into it.

To more easily and quickly tap into the power of the Law of Abundance and the Law of Attraction, we must remain diligent in our daily practice. This is especially important for the brief times in our lives that we cannot easily find a lot to be grateful for. Be grateful anyway. Abundance can be hidden from view at times. We must seek it out. Practicing gratitude is a strong method in discovering hidden abundance.

Practice Allowing

It is a spiritual principle, that we have received before we have asked. We ask through prayer for that which has been offered to us already. God shows us the answer and then waits for us to ask the question.

This is a deep spiritual awakening for many of us. It is the ultimate core truth behind dream manifestation. The key is in believing it is already there.

Some believe this is a spiritual or religious truth. Others believe that it is natural law. But here's the idea. There is one Great Creator and we aren't it. God puts a dream on our hearts and in our souls before we can imagine it. We discover the dream. We were not the origin of it. Therefore, it follows that if it is God's intention; then it exists before it enters our awareness. We are praying to receive what we have already been offered. Therefore, we have already received it. Our job is to allow it to manifest in our life.

Other Dream Doers talk about this all the time. They allow their dreams to manifest because they know that the dream is there and meant to be. They have directly experienced this simple truth and so they freely share the power of the message. Believing that our dream is waiting for us is an exciting and powerful expression of faith and it empowers us to continue with our full efforts in manifesting that which we envision.

It is in the nature of dreams, that once we begin to pray for them to manifest, God manifests them at that very moment in time.

"Therefore I say to you, whatever things you ask when you pray, believe that you receive them, and you will have them." Mark 11:24

By the time we are in Dream Doing, we have a belief in our dreams. It is really time to allow them to manifest. We pray and ask God to help us allow the dream to become a physical reality.

Our job then is to get from praying to receiving and we do this by believing first. Faith tells us that God has moved and that our dream now exists. Faith must keep us moving forward because we know that God has ALREADY provided it. Our only job in allowing is to let go of any efforts to control outcome.

In gratitude we give thanks for the manifestation ahead of time. If we have faith that our dreams are there, just waiting for us, then we need to practice gratitude now. In this way we will gain the spiritual and creative strength we need to chase our dreams and make them a reality. Remember, it already exists. We are in a place where all we need to do is to get from here- to there. Also remember that God is going to show us HOW. God is the one who makes the way.

It is in the nature of dreams that if we allow ourselves to now image or visualize Dream Living, that this powerful tool will guide us into final manifestation.

Once again, this is not a new tool. It has been used for centuries and continues to be highly effective. People who visualize success get success. People who "see" failure, "get" failure. Whatever we see in our minds is what we will find on the road ahead. As soon as we start to live our dreams in our minds; we find ourselves on a faster track in achieving them.

Norman Vincent Peale dedicated a book, *Positive Imaging*. to the power of positive thinking combined with imaging. As Peale reveals in his book, imaging reflects the faith and belief that our dream already exists. Peale reminds us that the combination of prayer, positive thinking and imaging will lead us to success. Our mind must not deviate from our positive images of our detailed Dream Doing.

Contributors to *The Secret* link visualization to the Law of Attraction, also tying into the idea that visualization reflects a belief that our dreams already exist. In fact, the major premise behind The Secret is the idea that our dreams manifest at the moment we ask for them. Visualization then, is an act that invokes the powerful Law of

Attraction. The universe that is energy; holds back nothing. We will attract all that we "see" and therefore believe we will find.

Joel Osteen in *Your Best Life* Now consistently reminds us to keep envisioning our success in dream living. With the same conviction as all of the others, he states that there is nothing in the world that can keep us from getting what we see. If we hold tight to our vision, we will receive it. In Even Eagles Need a Push, author David McNally suggests that visualization allows us the freedom to create dreams that are free of constraints and boundaries. In this sense, we are now freely tapping into the Law of Abundance. Julia Cameron suggests (among many other tools) creating a dream journal, stating that the act of writing out our dreams helps us to visualize and manifest them.

Let me suggest one additional powerful role of visualization. I believe that God allows us to see glimpses of our dreams for many reasons. My experience with imaging has led me to refine my dreams; which then led to bigger and more specific prayer. I also believe that by allowing me to "see" parts of my dream, I walk with less fear because it is known to me. I feel, as I see my dreams that I am increasingly deserving of them. And so, as I visualize, I find myself engaging in more gratitude and positive thinking knowing that as doors open, I have the visual, which will help guide me in future decision-making. Since I have seen the dream, I know what I am seeking.

Visualization is widely used in sports and education as an effective tool to gain success in achieving goals. Religious and spiritual traditions consistently reinforce the power of faith related to our vision. Imaging is an act of belief. It is doing the receiving because we believe it exists already. The list of believers and doers in visualization or imaging practices is endless. Whether we believe that this is a spiritual law or a natural law becomes irrelevant. Pray (Ask)- then Believe- and only then we shall Receive. Allow the dream to emerge in your mind.

It is in the nature of Dream Doing, that we would be wise to increase our practice of visualizing as we first chase, and then start doing our dreams.

Let me suggest that the more that we create a detailed picture of dream living in our minds, the easier it will be to find it. Imaging is seeking something that we believe can be found. We no longer are thinking of our dreams as a hopeful possibility. We start to see our vision as reality. We start to feel it. If we image or visualize hard enough and long enough, we will find it. Unconsciously, our intuition will guide us towards novel ways to create a physical manifestation that represents our focus. The power of a positive mind is formidable.

During Dream Weaving and Dream Catching, we experienced fleeting visions of our dreams and all the ways they might "look". In Dream Chasing and Dream Doing, we need to create an image that is visual and detailed. With each new idea, we create a bigger picture. Make it vivid. In fact, Peale suggests that we create it in 3-D. The more detailed we become, the more focused we will be. The power of the process of visualization is immense.

To increase the effect of imaging, I would suggest adding our vision to our daily gratitude list. Write down every new specific detail. Thank God each time you visualize and live your dream in your mind.

The Nature of Control- Leaving the Details to God

It is in the nature of dreams that there is a spiritual law of surrender. In surrender, we learn to turn it over to God.

Our job in allowing our dreams into our lives is to surrender our fears. When we open the door to allowing, we are called to surrender any human pretense of control. We come to realize that the How is answered continually through open doors, intuitive moments, and creative possibilities. We turn over the How to God and let Him take care of the details.

We are called to surrender the litany of fears that lead us towards any attempts to limit what we will accept. We are called to stop acting as children- saying that "We" get to decide "what we want, how we want it and when we want it." We are asked to surrender control and then practice patience, trust and faith in all that will be given to us.

How? and what if? are efforts at control, so that we might not feel our fear. By turning our fears over to God, we become empowered to use our energy more productively. In surrender, we find that what we are offered is bigger than what we conceived of in the first place. This is the gift of surrender. We learn the power of turning it over to God and letting Him do His job.

It is in the nature of dreams that Letting Go is an action that we must take and is an inherent part of the process.

The act of Letting Go is a process in and of itself. It is a spiritual practice; one that grows as we continue to use it. This is not a one-time deal. We start with moments of letting go, often with little things. As we practice in a small way, we gather the strength to increase our efforts. Letting go scares us. We want and we hope too much. Letting go of dreams, wishes and desires is difficult. Letting go of old stuff is difficult too. But, each time that we find that it works; our spiritual connection with God deepens and we let go of more and more.

It is in a sense a never-ending, ever increasing commitment to surrender our pretense of ultimate control over to God. We finally give up and turn it over to Him to do. We do our job, which is to listen to our intuition and follow it. We leave it up to God to guide us through our intuition and the physical universe. As we deepen our faith in surrender and letting go, our lives become more peaceful and more positive. We know that by allowing God to do His job, our lives will be better than we could ever possibly conceive, much less achieve. We don't have control over God or the Universe He created. Letting Go sets us free.

It is in the nature of dreams, that non-attachment to outcome reflects belief in spiritual intentions.

Non-attachment to outcome is not giving up. It is not only going so far and then saying- o.k. God, I'll turn it over to you now.

Visualization and imaging allowed us to walk in the "Big Picture". The big picture is bigger than we are.

Non-attachment to outcome is not giving up on a dream; it is a commitment to "*knowing*" that the dream will be manifested as long as we continue to do our part. We must continue to do, act, create, work, and walk forward, step-by-step. The outcome we are detaching from is our **finite** definition of what that dream looks like.

There are many options available for our dreams to be manifested and we certainly cannot know them all. Non-attachment to outcome is a willingness to be open to the manifestation of intent that God is providing us. It is natural that as we work towards achieving our dreams, that we become very attached to our own vision of what they will "look like".

We are not walking away from our dreams at all. Instead, we are detaching from I want what I want, when I want it, how I want it – and thank you very much by the way mentality. We are detaching from fear and focusing on faith.

The Energy in Dream Doing

It is often in the nature of Dream Doing that answers naturally, gently and then peacefully emerge.

In quiet times of deep reflection answers form and emerge in a very peaceful and unassuming way. There is a knowingness deep within that this is the right course of action. The energy is not chaotic, jarring, or negative. Dreams are not naturally "of fear"; any fear that we feel comes from us and is then placed upon the dream. The "What If" worry pattern is obsessive and therefore, fear-based energy. We may obsess and still achieve our dreams of course, but it just makes the process more painful and will often hamper our connection to our intuition. Fear may not keep us from our dreams, but it certainly can delay them. It interferes with the positive flow of energy. It only occurs when we are "out of" faith and trust. We are best served by trying to remain balanced with some sense of emotional calm.

It is in the nature of dreams, that positive energy has an ebb and flow to it. Always available of course, but we must experience the entire flow.

There are times of high energy and times of peaceful quiet, and times of patient practice, and times of fast and furious. Dreams are about life, in all of its complete nature. As we recognize the energy flow within ourselves, we will always be moving forward no matter how we feel. We may not see anything happening, yet spiritually everything is happening. We may feel that there are no open doors, yet the Universe is clearly beginning to open new ones.

During all periods of Dream Doing, something is happening. If we feel that we are encountering difficulty, then we must believe it is for our own good and continued growth. Obstacles may exist so that we become increasingly ready to receive bigger things. Hard times happen because we need to learn something, and the lesson learned will enhance our lives.

Difficult times are just that- difficult. They are not insurmountable. If they have been given to us, then it is only because we have the strength to carry on, learn what we must learn and come out the other side, better for it. Ebb and flow in a spiritual sense are positive and result in our own personal growth. We may not like it at the time, and we may get tired and frustrated but it is a natural part of achieving More.

It is in the nature of dreams, especially in Dream Doing- that sometimes an obstacle exists just to show us a new way of achieving our goals.

There are times we feel that we cannot approach one more obstacle. Dreams require work and commitment. We may feel exhausted from the effort. We feel as if there is nothing left inside us to give. This is part of the process. Successful Dream Doers have learned to rest, but not quit. On the other side of fatigue and feelings of hopelessness lies a new surge of creative energy. We rest, step back, and allow ourselves to approach an obstacle in a brand new way. Dream Doing represents growth and change. Obstacles give us the opportunity to achieve that.

Whenever we are faced with an obstacle, our minds are thrown into an unbalanced state. We are in disequilibrium, or cognitive dissonance; as it is sometimes called. It is part of our make-up that we cannot remain off balance; we seek intellectually to solve the problem in order to get back into a balanced state of mind.

According to the constructivist psychologists, there are only three possible cognitive responses to any perceived obstacle or problem.

Assimilation

Our first natural attempt is to use what we know to solve the problem. Sometimes this works and so we assimilate or absorb that successful experience into our history of problem solving and move on.

In some cases, what we know doesn't work. If we try to solve the problem time after time, using only what we know, we have just entered the classic definition of insanity. Insanity is doing the same thing over and over again, each time, expecting a different result.

When we are hitting our heads against a brick wall, over and over and over again and the problem isn't solved we tend to criticize our efforts. We think we are not praying deeply enough, or believing big enough, or striving hard enough. In fact, we did everything we could think of and it still didn't work. This is an opportunity to learn a new way of doing things. It is, in effect; an **Open Door**.

Accommodation

The second step that we take is to step back, look at the problem, and generate new possible ways to solve it. This is called accommodation. We accommodate by trying something new. Often, this is the time when Dream Weaving can help us achieve our goals. Because it is intuitive, spiritual and relies wholly on creative energy-the possibilities that emerge are often enough to lead us to a new way of looking at the problem. We succeed, because we just looked at life from a different perspective. We have grown in our ability to face new challenges and to succeed in over-coming them.

Walking Away

The only other option we have is to give up. That is the third way to bring us back to balance or cognitive equilibrium. We walk away. At times, we try accommodation and still cannot find a solution. We walk away because we have the sense that this is a problem best left alone at this point in time.

Other times, we either don't try a new way, or barely try and then quit anyway. We give up before we searched the possibilities for a novel solution. We cannot leave our comfort zone. We are afraid of change. In this case, the problem generally pops up again in the future as the Universe searches to teach us a new way to overcome.

Dream Doing generally will require cognitive accommodation at certain times along the way. We will be thrown off balance. We will face new situations. It will lead us through challenging times. Be prepared realizing that we have been provided with one more open door, and that there is a meaningful purpose for us to be there.

It is in the nature of dreams that they are subject to the creative energy of the synergistic effect.

In all acts of creation, natural and man-made; we see evidence of the synergistic effect. Put simply, the synergistic effect states that the whole is greater than the sum of all of its parts. Take a look at your body. Your essence, your wholeness, your uniqueness is bigger than groups of cells added together. Dreams are bigger than the sum of each ounce of energy or creative thought that goes into them.

In Dream Doing, what this means is that for every step we take towards achieving our dream; the Universe through God takes two steps towards fulfilling it. The energy created by each step is bigger than we alone can generate. Energy releases additional energy- the product is bigger and greater than the sum of all effort that we put into it. Synergistic energy is creative energy and therefore positive and subject to the Law of Attraction.

Commitment and Dream Doing

It is in the nature of Dream Doing that we will need to commit over and over again.

This is especially true with our biggest dreams, but clearly each dream requires a commitment to bring it to completion. Each time we commit we add positive energy to the dream. This positive energy increases our strength, clarity, intent and knowingness. Each step in commitment is one step closer to realization. Each act of re-commitment carries with it synergistic energy. It builds and multiplies in its power.

As we increase our commitment to actualizing our dreams, we should use the powerful tools of visualization or imaging once again. At this point we should also increase the level of our practice. We become more and more specific as we see and visualize our new lives. Every minute detail begins to emerge. The more specific we become in our visualization, the closer we come to realization.

We move into right brain visualization techniques, we write out specific details of what we expect, we create story boards, or posters, play a movie of our dream life in our minds or create prayer journals that detail our manifestation. The more we visualize or image ourselves living our dreams, the more vested we become in achieving them.

There will be a point where we turn the corner and feel compelled to finish. Our dreams start drawing us in as we visualize more. Energy increases along with our focus, determination and perseverance. Commitment increases as belief increases and the powerful Law of Attraction moves back in to support our efforts.

Then there will come a day that our commitment is so strong and so directed that nothing can stop us because we have committed from the depths of our soul. We do not allow anyone or anything to get in our way. There is no turning back. At this point, we are generally on the verge of achieving our vision. We are now at a place where we will go to any lengths to live the life of our dreams.

The Home Stretch

It is in the nature of Dream Doing, that there will come
a time when we start to doubt and think of quitting.

In the beginning as we weave and catch we flesh out our ideas; we create a plan, product, picture or outline of our dreams. *We are doing-* and everything flows. We are excited in the act of creating the dream that is emerging.

Then we hit it- the inevitable period of fear and doubt. It is the hump- but it can become a brick wall. We feel that we are getting nowhere and that nothing is happening. We stop.

Dream Doing often has the last hurtle phase. We stumble, we rest, we reflect, we question the validity or the value of continuing on. We feel that we are not ready or the time is not right or that things are not flowing as easily as they should.

This is the giving up phase of Dream Doing. It comes just as we are getting ready to finish and make the final commitment. This is natural and normal because we are facing the unknown. It is often risky and it is a time when we may feel as if we are taking the great leap of faith without a safety net.

This is the time when dreams are moving into the test of reality. It comes just as we are getting ready to finish and make the final commitment for that reason. We fear that they won't work, our joy in creation will only lead to dashed hopes- that we will 'look' bad or foolish in our pursuits.

It is here that we have to gather all our inner strength. We need to face our fear, accept it and then move forward and do it anyway. This is the period of testing our faith in our dreams and trust in our self. *The most difficult part of Dream Doing is to hold on to the intuitive belief that we are right, despite the odds against us.* When we respect ourselves, we respect our dreams and we respect our God. This does not mean that it is easy. It means that we may need to fight for it.

On a positive note, this happens to each and every one of us. It's part of the process of completion. It means that we are at the end of one stage and the beginning of the next. *It is crossing over into action.*

To fulfill our dreams we cannot afford to straddle two worlds; the world of safety in silent planning and the world of unknown actual testing of the dream. Full commitment is required to get through the obstacles in our way.

We truly fear the death of our dream, which is one of the most painful experiences we can imagine. We feel we should wait, we are not ready, the dream needs more work, we need more time, money, support, etc. We feel that if we wait, we can hold onto our dreams a bit longer and not risk losing them.

We will kill the dream if we stay here too long. It will fade into obscurity- losing power and momentum. We must not allow ourselves to stop. We can slow down. We can rest. We can take a break. But we cannot quit. When we turn our back on our soul filled dreams; we also turn our back on our self and our God.

It is in the nature of dreams that we must face our fear again and again in The Home Stretch.

O.K.- here we are- all of a sudden everything is moving quickly. People, places, things...support for our dreams keeps pouring in. The pace of it all is frightening. We feel as if we are being catapulted forward, as though we are caught in the current of the fierce, flowing river and suddenly all we want to do is back paddle.

Dream manifestation is around the corner- we can feel it, taste it, and smell it. Seeing it takes our breath away- the changes that are occurring become huge in our minds. All change is stressful, even positive change. To realize that is our key to successful maneuvering through the home stretch. Wanting to slow down the pace is only our need for ultimate control.

We have been seeking and now we are finding the answer. Feel the fear and then walk through to the other side of it. Don't get in your own way; don't throw rocks on the path ahead.

The home stretch often requires that final huge step of commitment. Others may not support us, in their own fear of what they cannot see. We cannot let their fear in, simply because it only serves to increase our own. We start thinking of the serenity of the status quo, of the old days, of the possibility of keeping the old along with the new.

Dream Doing is a spiritual process, and much like healing will be full of goodbyes as much as it will be full of hellos. We will, in the home stretch be closing doors behind us, so that we are free to walk through the open doors that come our way. Dream Doing is soaring with the eagles, we cannot carry a lot of past baggage on our wings- or we won't be able to fly free.

Our final commitment requires us to take that leap of faith. We are testing what was previously a hopeful possibility. We are bringing our dreams out into the light. The only dreams worth achieving are the dreams we fight for.

When we win and find ourselves living our dreams- we cherish them deeply, we respect ourselves highly and we live in the passion we truly deserve. We must move forward in trust and faith in our self and our God. This is the last mile and the hardest one to walk. It is the place where many people give up, just before their dreams are realized. We can choose to be the ones who cross over to the side of Dream Living.

My Dream Chasing, Dream Doing Web

Establishing Dream Partnerships
Create an Intimacy Map

Sociologists, psychologists and others have used this method for years to establish relationship patterns. In the innermost circle, start writing the names of those you are most intimate with. The farther out you move on the circles, the less intimacy you share with the people in that circle. When you are done, circle any names of possible dream partners.

Practice Containment
This idea comes from Julia Cameron, The Artist's Way

Creative energy can "spill" right out of us, especially when we are in the Creative Process.

Dreams have no boundaries; but Dream Doing requires that we establish them for ourselves. We cannot "waste" creative energy- there is only so much we can "leak out" without leaching our system and depleting it.

Certain people, places and activities leach our personal energy and so we must identify them and then practice containment through establishing rules, boundaries and limitations. On the other hand, certain people, places and activities feed our creative energy- for example, in a give and take with other positive Dream Doers, we gain energy from each other; we don't lose it. List all positive sources of energy outside the Jar.

Using your intimacy web as well as other tools- fill up your Containment Jar with a list of who and what depletes you. Then establish a plan to create boundaries and minimize the damage.

My Containment Jar

My Action Plan

Daily Objectives

Weekly Objectives

Week 1

Week 2

Week 3

Week 4

Month 1 Goals

Month 2 Goals

Month 3 Goals

Month 4 Goals

Short Term Plan

Long Term Plan

Asset Recovery and Gratitude List

Dear God,

I am so grateful today that you gifted me with_____

_____

I am so grateful today that you gifted me with_____

_____

I am so grateful today that you gifted me with_____

_____

I am so grateful today that you gifted me with_____

_____

I am so grateful today that you gifted me with_____

_____

I am so grateful today that you gifted me with_____

_____

I am so grateful today that you gifted me with_____

_____

I am so grateful today that you gifted me with_____

_____

I am so grateful today that you gifted me with_____

_____

Faith

Sylvia Lehtinen~ a great counselor and friend
once described the relationship between fear
and faith to me in a very visual way...
Faith is when you are standing in the
middle of a minefield. All is hidden, and
you must walk through to the other side.
Faith says that you know, that no matter
what happens, you will still be alright.....

What Landmines Line Your Minefield Today?

Dream Doing Tree of Abundance
Where There Is No Way- God Makes a Way

Take your list of fears and landmines and create a visual image of God taking care of each and every one. Celebrate what you see by placing all of what you are receiving on the Tree of Abundance. You are at the last step of achieving your dreams. Our God will provide the Way. Celebrate that with this tree that will remind you daily of all that is coming. Now you can "See It".

DREAM DOING
Current Obstacles in My Path
And
All Possible Ways of Solving the Problem
(by going over, under, through,
around, or by waiting)

Reminder- don't forget to go back to Dream Weaving to generate your possible list. Use your creative side, to create the solution your left-brain hasn't "thought of" yet. If your LB had the answer, the obstacle wouldn't be on your list!

"For every problem, there is always
a solution- ALWAYS"
We may not LIKE IT- but it is there
When we do not LIKE a Possible Solution
We have the Choice to Decide.
I CAN'T OR I WON'T
We can say- "I Can't..." or we can
choose to say "I Won't. ...".

I can't is the language of the victim, who believes that little is under their control.

I won't is the powerful language of the Dream Doer, who understands free will and free choice and is willing to take responsibility for the consequences of the actions that result from choice. Dream Doers always respect and retain the power of personal choice. Looking at your possibility list- if you cross something off of it- is it really that you can't choose that option, or is it because you won't choose that option. Reflect in total honesty before you respond.

Open Doors and Closed Doors

List every Open Door- each positive event that has occurred in your life.

Start with your childhood and then continue on...
remember big doors as well as the small ones.
Remember that Doors Open through the Universe of
people, places and things that God sets in our path.
We all have a rich and plentiful history of Open Doors,
it is important to remember and recognize each one.

Now List all the Doors that have Opened since
you started Dream Weaving, Dream Catching,
Dream Chasing and Dream Doing

Closed Doors

**List any Doors that appear to be Closed
to you at this point in time.**

Dream Weaving~ Dream Catching

Dream Chasing~ Dream Doing

Is....

About action and Responsible Choice
A source of positive driving energy
Is consuming
Is creative
Is trusting
Is deliberate
Is open
Is energizing
Is determined
Is resilient
Is focused
Is joyful
Is affirming

The Process
Is about feeling right, or alright in the world,
things make sense
Is finally visualized
Becomes real and doable in our minds
Gives us the freedom we seek
Supports the risks we choose to take
Is about faith
Is a reflection of the body of hope
Is creative
Is challenging
Gives our intuition its voice~ a big booming voice
Is intimate
Is personal

Is honest
Is about living in our own truth
Is about intimacy
Is the source of generativity
Is a process that starts at birth and continues until
the day we die.

NOTES

REFERENCES AND RESOURCES

This is not an extensive list, it is a compilation of all of the books that I have used most heavily in developing this book, as well as a few other good ones! I offer this annotated bibliography for those who would like to continue to read about aspects of Dream Doing. Enjoy!

Beattie, Melody. _More Language of Letting Go: 366 New Daily Meditations._ MN: Hazelden. 2000.

Wonderful daily meditations followed by short prayer. Strong spiritual approach which mentions dream recovery, visualization, letting go, gratitude, trust and timing as well as other subjects involved in Dream Doing.

Author of _The Language of Letting Go, Codependent No More, Playing it By Heart_ as well as other great texts.

Byrne, Rhonda. _The Secret._ NY: Atria Books, 2006.

If you haven't done so- this is a wonderful book to read. A compilation of essays from 25 teachers of the secret, this book defines the laws of the Universe. Featured topics include The Law of Attraction, The Law of Abundance, gratitude, the role of expectation, Ask-Believe-Receive, visualization and the power of our own thoughts. A clear presentation of Natural Law. An easy and fun read.

Bleivernicht, Melanie. <u>Walking Faith Forward: Perspectives of Ordinary Life Transformed by Faith.</u> NY: iUniverse, Inc. 2007.

This weekly devotional presents topics related to honest free choice, the spiritual use of the word "no", etc. and follows each devotional with a weekly focus for a plan of action in our own lives. Scriptural references related to each topic are shared at the end of the chapters.

Cameron, Julia. <u>The Artist's Way: A Spiritual Path to Higher Creativity.</u> NY: Jeremy P. Tarcher/ Putnam, 2002.

Do not let the title fool you, this is a book for all dream doers, since it is about creating a creative lifestyle. Whether we dream of writing, art, knitting, crocheting, painting, woodworking, parenting, designing a kitchen, a business, a new tomorrow, etc.- all dreams are a true reflection of the art of creation. This book is about getting to a place where we can create our own dreams. It is about the journey back to the basics of dream recovery. Spiritually driven, this book includes the following topics: Recovery of ...... safety, Identity, power, integrity, possibility, the law of abundance, a sense of connection, strength, compassion, self-protection, autonomy and faith. It is a training manual, full of tips and exercises to help us on our way. Julia Cameron remains one of my greatest inspirations, and so I hope that you may consider reading this book.

Cameron, Julia. <u>Walking in this World: The Practical Art of Creativity.</u> NY: Jeremy P. Tarcher/ Penguin Group, 2002.

Once again, a very strong spiritual approach to creative living when we declare that we are, in fact; an artist. As a writer and teacher, this is one of my most favorite books. Topics include basic tools, so necessary to living a balanced life, Morning Pages, The Artist's Date, and Weekly Walks as well as the following: Discovery... of who we are, where we have been, and where we are going. Contents of chapters are a sense of.... Origin, perspective, proportion, adventure, personal territory, boundaries, momentum, discernment, resiliency, camaraderie, authenticity and finally dignity. A real must read for any RB creative in order that we receive the gifts of validation, support and true understanding.

Cloud, Henry & Townsend, John. _God Will Make a Way: What to Do When You Don't Know What to Do._ TN: Thomas Nelson, 2006.
 Great book with scriptural references includes topics such as choosing our traveling companions, how to deal with toxic relationships, leaving our past in our past, dealing with limitations and obstacles in our path. A great discussion of partnerships. Authors of several additional books including _Boundaries._

Dyer, Wayne W. _The Power of Intention: Learning to Co-Create Your World Your Way._ CA: Hay House, Inc., 2004.
 The author of many spiritual works, in this book Dr. Dyer presents the view of intention as related to the field of energy that exists in the universe. He offers a step-by-step approach towards bring the seven faces of intention-(kindness, creativity, love, beauty, expansion, abundance, and reception) to all aspects of our life. This includes self-respect, success, purpose, relationships, healing, etc. Dyer has authored several spiritual books.

Gelb, Micheal J. _How to Think Like Leonardo da Vinci: Seven Steps to Genius Every Day._ NY: Bantam Dell, 2004.
 Micheal Gelb writes a very interesting and exciting book, full of great ideas and exercises that will help guide us in developing a more balanced and productive lifestyle as we chase our dreams. Among the topics included is a discussion of right brain- left brain dominance and balance, the power of incubation of ideas in dream doing, mind mapping, the role of curiosity, emotional intelligence, internal motivation, willingness in all forms, the balanced life of integrating our body, mind, heart and soul in a spiritual sense as well as other topics that can challenge us in our own growth.

Jeffers, Susan. _Feel the Fear and Do it Anyway_. NY: Ballantine Books, 2007.

This piece of work is all about fear, something each and every one of us lives through. Dr. Jeffers presents a very straightforward and insightful rendition of all that we fear as well as stories and methods of walking through fear in a way that all of us can easily relate to. This book is about change- and therefore challenges us to think, and therefore act- differently. A lot of information in an easy read format.

Jeffers, Susan. _End the Struggle and Dance With Life: How to Build Yourself Up When the World Gets You Down_. NY: St. Martins Press, 1996.

A spiritual approach to living life whole, Dr. Jeffers presents her ideas regarding critical issues such as trust, letting go in general, letting go specifically of our own expectations, the spiritual key to success, non-perfectionism, purpose, excess baggage, free will (choice), and the power to live our own lives. Many easily doable activities that support healing and growth.

McNally, David. _Even Eagles Need a Push: Learning to Soar in a Changing World._ NY: Dell Publishing Group, Inc. 1994.

This is a great, spiritual and direct approach to achieving our dreams. The author presents a clear, easy, straightforward way to accomplish much of Dream Doing. Topics include establishing mission and purpose, asset discovery, the importance of what we believe and how we feel and the huge power of commitment in achieving our biggest dreams. Full of quotes, activities and stories that we can easily relate to. A simply written book that each of us can understand combined with a powerful message. A great read.

Osteen, Joel. _Your Best Life Now: 7 Steps to Living at Your Full Potential._ NY: Faith Words, 2004.

Joel Osteen presents many of the ideas that are found in this workshop including God's favor, vision, limiting beliefs, receiving only what we expect, letting go of the past, self fulfilling prophecy, the power of positive support, the amazing power of our own thoughts, dreams, and increasing our level of requests of what we expect from God.

Peale, Norman Vincent. The Power of Positive Thinking and The Amazing Results of Positive Thinking. NY: Simon & Schuster, 2005- Fireside Edition.

This in my mind is the most definitive work in the field of positive thinking. A classic since it was first published- it is full of true stories, scriptural reference and is tied very closely to establishing a deeper connection with God through a prayerful life. Norman Vincent Peale really tells it how it is....

Peale, Norman Vincent. Positive Imaging: The Powerful Way to Change Your Life. NY: Random House, 1982

Clearly written book about the power of imaging or visualization. Also presents the idea that once visualized, the dream already exists. Ties imaging into all aspects of our lives including self-esteem, money, health, marriage, etc. with scriptural references throughout the book.

Quezada, Adolfo. Loving Yourself for God's Sake. NY: Resurrection Press, 1997.

A little book with a strong spiritual message. This book covers topics relating to self-love, God love, self-esteem, self-responsibility, letting go of the past, the meaning and purpose of our lives and generativity. A really great and easy yet, thought provoking read.

Seamands, David A. Healing for Damaged Emotions. CO: Cook Communications Ministries, 2002.

This is a book that speaks from a Christian perspective about the deepest of healing- much of it due to childhood trauma. Sections with scriptural references include a focus of the addiction known as perfectionism, as well as depression, self-esteem, asking to be healed, forgiveness of self and others, and the process of healing from a strong faith-based approach.

Wilkinson, Bruce. <u>The Prayer of Jabez: Breaking Through to the Blessed Life.</u> OR: Multnomah Publishers, Inc. 2000.
This little book presents the power of a simple prayer that urges us to Pray Big and then Pray even Bigger. This is a book that reflects on the power of Asking and relates it to the story of Jabez. He also brings in God's favor, abundance etc. and relates to other scriptural references. An easy read, a powerful book full of positive affirmation for fulfilling our dreams.

Zukav, Gary & Francis, Linda. <u>The Heart of the Soul: Emotional Awareness.</u> NY: Simon and Schuster. 2001.
This is a book about authentic living, coming to understand our emotional selves, understanding how we process energy, and addressing the source of our emotional pain, so as to move from survival into a greater spiritual life.
Zukav is the author of several other books including <u>The Dancing Wu Li Masters: An Overview of the New Physics,</u> <u>The Seat of the Soul</u> and <u>Soul Stories.</u>

As Always: <u>The Bible</u>

Printed in the United States
By Bookmasters